GW00726808

A note to the student ...

This book represents a brand new concept in revision guides, and allows you, the student to learn in a combination of different ways ...

'Big Picture' Concept Map   1

Before each section there is a 'Big Picture' page that connects the main ideas and information in the section. This means you can jump about from idea to idea within a topic. This is good for everyone but especially those people who like to know how everything fits together before they start to look at all the different bits.

Structured Sequence   2

The pages within the section present the information in appropriate steps and sequences using words, colours and pictures as 'memory pegs' to increase the amount that you remember.

Simple Summary Statements   3

Each section ends with a summary page which reviews and consolidates the work you have just covered by concentrating simply on the main ideas. This enables you to 'Hang Memories' from short, simple statements.

All the pages work together to give you a 'WHOLE BRAIN' LEARNING EXPERIENCE.

In short the information you need to help you succeed in your examination ...

... has been LINKED TOGETHER to give you an <u>overall picture</u> of each section ...

... has been CLEARLY SEQUENCED, to help you learn by <u>reading</u> ...

... can be TAPED ONTO A WALKMAN from the summary to help you learn by <u>listening</u> and ...

... can be WRITTEN OUT FROM THE SUMMARY and/or BIG PICTURE to help you to learn by <u>doing</u>.

This approach to learning gives your brain the VARIED DIET of experiences that it needs.

This HELPS YOUR MEMORY to retain the key information which will GET YOU THE GRADES YOU WANT.

ALSO, HAVE A LOOK AT THE WORKBOOK THAT SUPPORTS THIS GUIDE.
IT CONTAINS A PAGE OF QUESTIONS FOR EVERY PAGE OF THE GUIDE FOR ONLY £1.50!

CONTENTS

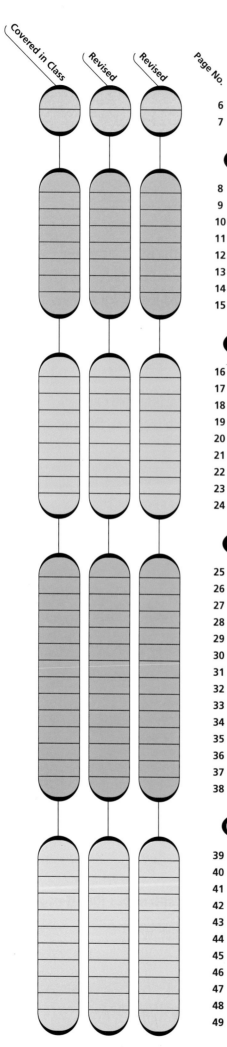

● CONTENTS

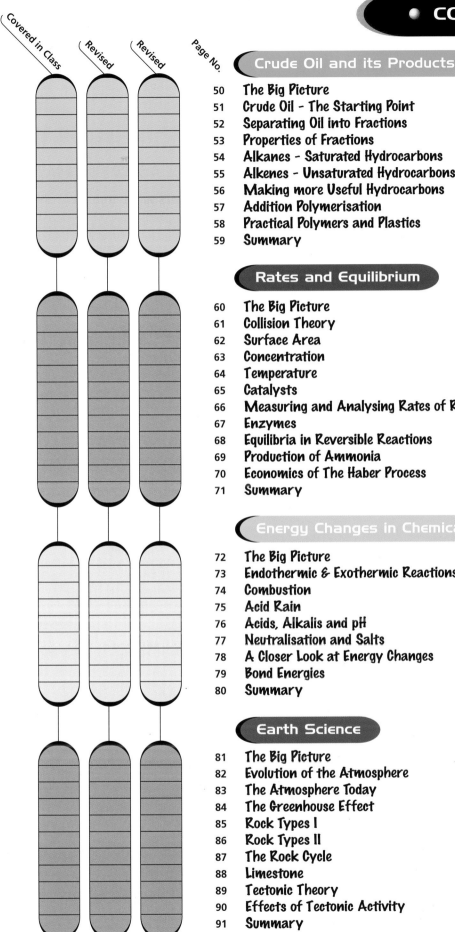

- Don't just read! LEARN ACTIVELY!

- Constantly test yourself ... WITHOUT LOOKING AT THE BOOK.

- When you have revised a small sub-section or a diagram, PLACE A BOLD TICK AGAINST IT. Similarly, tick the "progress and revision" section of the contents when you have done a
- page. This is great for your self confidence.

- Jot down anything which will help YOU to remember - no matter how trivial it may seem.

- DON'T BE TEMPTED TO HIGHLIGHT SECTIONS WITH DIFFERENT COLOURS. TOO MUCH COLOUR REDUCES CLARITY AND CAUSES CONFUSION. YOUR EXAM WILL BE IN BLACK AND WHITE!

- These notes are highly refined. Everything you need is here, in a highly organised but user-friendly format. Many questions depend only on STRAIGHTFORWARD RECALL OF FACTS, so make sure you LEARN THEM.

- THIS IS YOUR BOOK! Use it throughout your course in the ways suggested and your revision will be both organised and successful.

HIGHER/SPECIAL TIER

Material, identified by the major syllabuses as being HIGHER/SPECIAL TIER is enclosed in a red box.

CONSULTANT EDITORS ...

- **Stephen Tierney** - Formerly Head of Science at De La Salle, St. Helens.

    Currently Deputy Head at Our Lady's Catholic High School, Lancaster.

- **Rachel Dick** - Chemistry teacher at St. Aidan's Church of England High School, Harrogate.

NOTES

Your Science coursework will involve you doing an investigation. We have chosen as our example a rates of reaction investigation between Calcium Carbonate and Hydrochloric Acid.

Calcium + Hydrochloric ⟶ Calcium + Carbon + Water
Carbonate   Acid   Chloride   Dioxide

$$CaCO_{3(s)} + 2HCl_{(aq)} \longrightarrow CaCl_{2(aq)} + CO_{2(g)} + H_2O_{(l)}$$

Stage I(a): Planning

- Work out which factors affect the rate of reaction. Decide on **one** to investigate.
- Write down a clear **prediction** and then use **scientific ideas** to explain the prediction you have made. You can use the section on Rates and Reaction from this revision guide to help you.
- Too many students don't get top marks because they rush this first part - don't you make this mistake!

Having worked out that the temperature and concentration of the Hydrochloric Acid or the particle size of the Calcium Carbonate may affect the rate of the reaction I have decided to investigate the effect of concentration.

Prediction: I think that as the concentration of the Hydrochloric Acid increases, the rate of reaction will also increase (Then explain your prediction using the Collision Theory. Why not include some drawings to help make your explanation. It is always a good idea to write a word and symbol equation for the reaction).

Stage I(b): More Planning

- Write down how you will carry out the experiments. Remember to include how you will make the test fair and safe.
- Plan to investigate **five values** for the variable you have chosen and to **repeat** your experiment (at least two sets of results are needed).
- Do some **preliminary work** to find out the most suitable concentrations of Hydrochloric Acid to use and the correct mass of Calcium Carbonate. Include your preliminary work in your final write-up, it will gain you extra marks.

Stage 2: Obtaining Evidence

- During your experimental work keep a careful note of all the measurements you make.
- Remember to measure accurately and to repeat your experiment.
- Your results are probably best presented in a table.

Concentration of Acid (M)	Time taken to obtain 50cm³ of Carbon Dioxide (secs)			
	Test 1	Test 2	Test 3	Average
0.5				
1.0				
1.5				
2.0				
2.5				

Five values of concentration used

Make sure you put in the **units** at the top of the table in the column heading. Do **not** repeat units down the columns.

To work out the average (mean) results:

$$\text{Average} = \frac{\text{Test 1} + \text{Test 2} + \text{Test 3}}{3}$$

Stage 3: Analysing Evidence And Drawing Conclusions

- Decide on the best way to indentify any trends in your results - use graphs.

- When drawing a line graph make sure you draw a line/curve of **"best fit"** (this is a line/curve with the points evenly balanced on each side).

- Spot any **anamolous results** (one's that do not fit the pattern - these are important later).

- Think of ways to analyse your results. For example Rate = $^1/$Time.

- In your conclusion write clearly any **patterns** you have identified from your results, say how these compare with your **original prediction** and explain the patterns using **scientific ideas** (if you have done your planning properly look back at what you wrote there!).

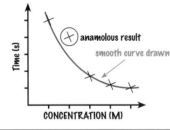

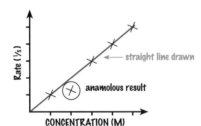

Always make sure that you **label** both your axes, and don't forget the **units**.

Stage 4: Evaluating Your Evidence

- This is the section that students find the most difficult, so lets take it step by step.

- First look back at your results. Comment on whether you got any **anamolous results** - look at both your test results and the averages.

- Try to give reasons why you got any anamolous results or why you didn't.

- Go carefully through the method you used. Try to think of whether the apparatus and method you used were the most accurate, or whether they could have been improved.

From the graphs, you can see that an anamolous result has been obtained for 1M concentration of Hydrochloric Acid (if you get something similar in your investigation try to give a reason why). Think about some of the apparatus you used and the method. Were all the marble chips you used the same size? Different sized chips will have slightly different surface areas. Sometimes gas can "escape" from a conical flask before the bung can be put in. This is particularly true when the rate of reaction is very fast at the beginning of the reaction. Some scientists avoid this by using a divided conical flask.

Divided conical flask

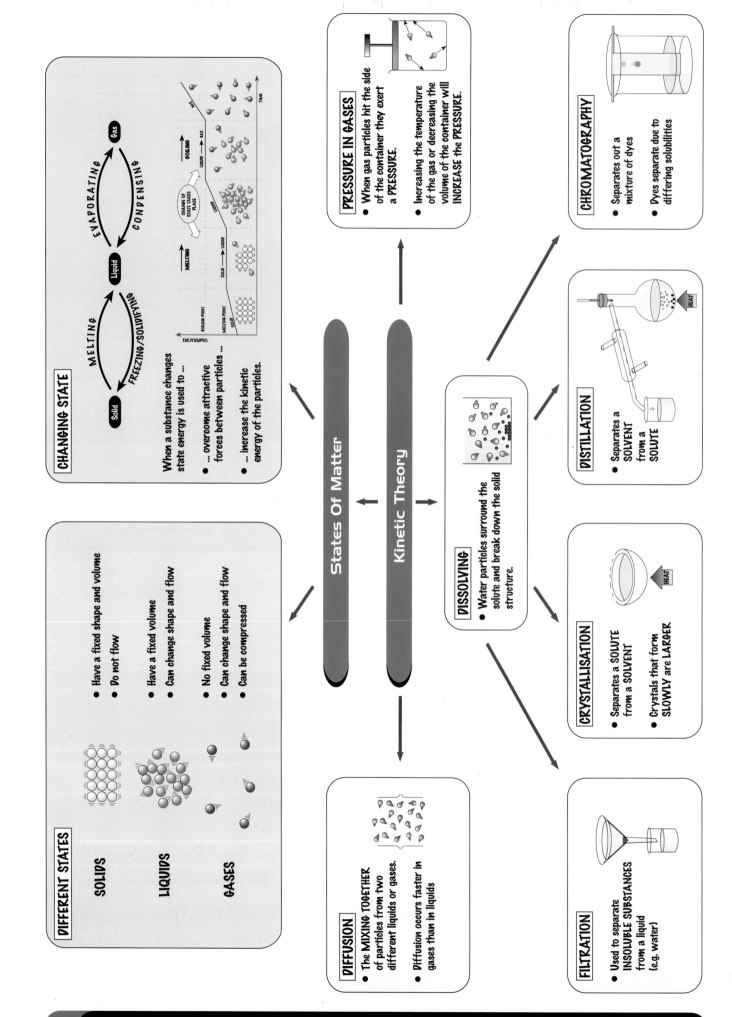

CHANGING STATE

EVAPORATING · CONDENSING
MELTING
FREEZING/SOLIDIFYING

Gas
Liquid
Solid

When a substance changes state energy is used to …

- … overcome attractive forces between particles …
- … increase the kinetic energy of the particles.

CHANGE OF STATE TAKES PLACE

BOILING · LIQUID → GAS
MELTING · SOLID → LIQUID
BOILING POINT
MELTING POINT
SOLID

TEMPERATURE · TIME

PRESSURE IN GASES

- When gas particles hit the side of the container they exert a PRESSURE.
- Increasing the temperature of the gas or decreasing the volume of the container will INCREASE the PRESSURE.

CHROMATOGRAPHY

- Separates out a mixture of dyes
- Dyes separate due to differing solubilities

DISTILLATION

- Separates a SOLVENT from a SOLUTE

HEAT

States Of Matter

Kinetic Theory

DIFFERENT STATES

SOLIDS
- Have a fixed shape and volume
- Do not flow

LIQUIDS
- Have a fixed volume
- Can change shape and flow

GASES
- No fixed volume
- Can change shape and flow
- Can be compressed

DISSOLVING

- Water particles surround the solute and break down the solid structure.

CRYSTALLISATION

- Separates a SOLUTE from a SOLVENT
- Crystals that form SLOWLY are LARGER

HEAT

DIFFUSION

- The MIXING TOGETHER of particles from two different liquids or gases.
- Diffusion occurs faster in gases than in liquids

FILTRATION

- Used to separate INSOLUBLE SUBSTANCES from a liquid (e.g. water)

There are three STATES OF MATTER ...
- ... SOLID, LIQUID and GAS.

The KINETIC THEORY OF MATTER states that ...
- ... matter is made up of VERY SMALL PARTICLES (atoms, molecules, ions) ...
- ... which are CONTINUALLY MOVING.
- The extent of this movement depends on their STATE ...
- ... and the TEMPERATURE they are at.

Solids

Particles are ...
- Arranged in a REGULAR PATTERN.
- VERY CLOSE TOGETHER and ...
- ... EACH PARTICLE exerts a STRONG FORCE OF ATTRACTION ...
- ... on every OTHER PARTICLE NEAR TO IT.

Particles can ...
- ONLY VIBRATE (move to and fro) ...
- ... about a FIXED POSITION.

Liquids

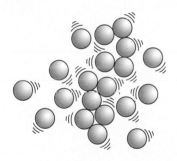

Particles are ...
- NOT in a REGULAR ARRANGEMENT.
- CLOSE TOGETHER and ...
- ... EACH PARTICLE exerts a SMALLER FORCE OF ATTRACTION ...
- ... on every OTHER PARTICLE NEAR TO IT.

Particles can ...
- MOVE AROUND ...
- ... in ANY DIRECTION ...
- ... and CHANGE PLACES with other particles in the liquid.

Gases

Particles are ...
- NOT in a REGULAR ARRANGEMENT.
- VERY FAR APART with LARGE SPACES between particles and ...
- ... there are almost NO FORCES OF ATTRACTION ...
- ... between the PARTICLES.

Particles can ...
- MOVE AROUND VERY QUICKLY ...
- ... in ANY DIRECTION ...
- ... within their container.

The PROPERTIES of the different states of matter can be explained using the KINETIC THEORY.

SOLIDS	LIQUIDS	GASES

SOLIDS

- HAVE A HIGH DENSITY

A SOLID of known volume

> The particles are very tightly packed together.

- CANNOT BE COMPRESSED

The SOLID in a syringe-like container

> The particles are very close together and won't go closer.

- DO NOT FLOW

> The particles are not able to move around and swap places.

- HAVE A FIXED SHAPE

SOLID in new container

> The particles are held in a set position by strong forces of attraction.

- HAVE A FIXED VOLUME

SOLID

> The strong forces of attraction keep the particles very close together.

LIQUIDS

- HAVE A MEDIUM DENSITY

The same volume of LIQUID in a beaker

> The particles are close together but not as close as in solids.

- CANNOT BE COMPRESSED

The LIQUID in a syringe-like container

> The particles are close together and won't go closer.

- CAN FLOW

> The particles can slide over and past each other.

- CAN CHANGE SHAPE

LIQUID in new container

> The particles can move past each other and take up the shape of the container.

- HAVE A FIXED VOLUME

LIQUID

> The forces of attraction keep the particles close together.

GASES

- HAVE A VERY LOW DENSITY

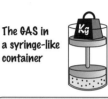

A GAS in the same beaker

> The particles are very far apart.

- CAN BE COMPRESSED

The GAS in a syringe-like container

> The particles can be forced closer together because they are far apart.

- CAN FLOW

> The particles can move past each other.

- CAN CHANGE SHAPE

GAS in new container

> The particles are moving very fast and fill any container they are put in.

- HAVE NO FIXED VOLUME

GAS

> The particles can move far away from each other because there are almost no forces of attraction.

- Also solids, liquids and gases ALL EXPAND WHEN HEATED as the particles gain energy and move further apart. They CONTRACT WHEN COOLED as the particles lose energy and move closer together.

 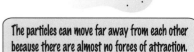

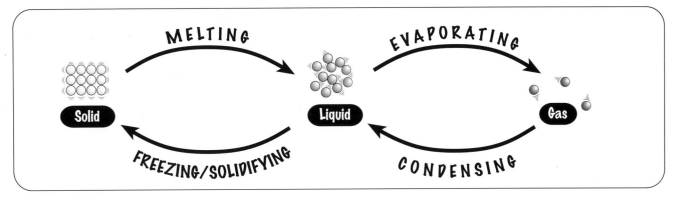

Heating Curves

When a solid substance is heated it changes to a liquid and then to a gas.
The HEAT ENERGY IS USED ... to OVERCOME THE FORCES OF ATTRACTION between particles and ...
... to give the PARTICLES MORE KINETIC (MOVEMENT) ENERGY (move faster!)

This graph shows the change in temperature of a substance when it is heated.
Look carefully at how the TEMPERATURE OF THE SUBSTANCE STAYS THE SAME WHEN IT IS
CHANGING STATE (even though it is still being heated).

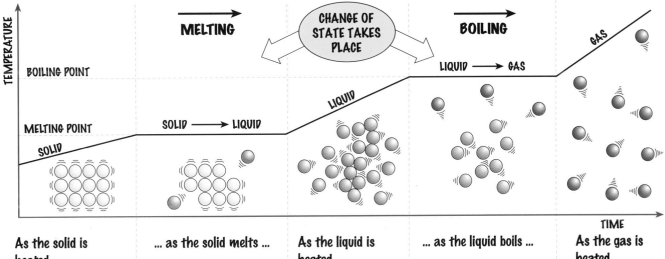

As the solid is heated ...

● ... the particles vibrate faster and faster.

● The strong attraction between the particles begins to break down until ...

... as the solid melts ...

● ... the particles move further apart ...

● ... and begin to move around.

● The heat energy is used to overcome strong forces of attraction between particles and increase their kinetic energy.

As the liquid is heated ...

● ... the particles move around faster and faster.

● Some particles begin to escape from the surface of the liquid until ...

... as the liquid boils ...

● ... many particles begin to escape from the surface of the liquid.

● The heat energy is used to overcome the forces of attraction between particles and increase their kinetic energy.

As the gas is heated ...

● ... the particles move around even faster.

If a gas is cooled down to a liquid and then to a solid you would get a mirror image of the graph above.

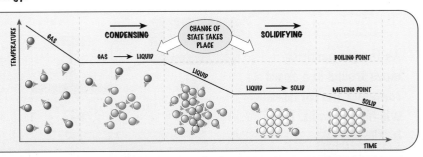

You may have noticed that if someone lets off a stink bomb or is wearing perfume the smell can soon spread around a room. The mixing together of the particles in two different gases or liquids is called DIFFUSION.

Diffusion In Gases

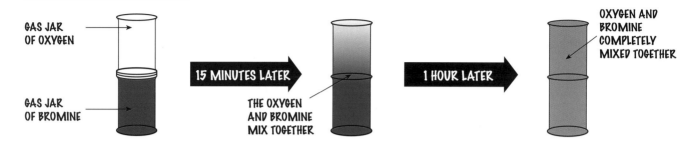

The KINETIC THEORY can explain this:

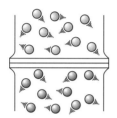

Particles in a gas are moving around very quickly.

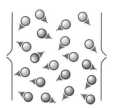

There are spaces between the particles that allow the gases to mix together ...

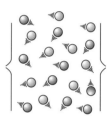

... until the particles are evenly spread between the two gas jars.

Diffusion In Liquids

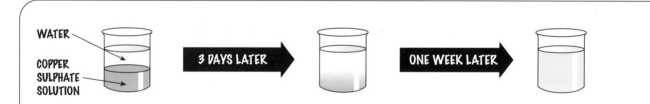

Diffusion in liquids is much slower than diffusion in gases because the particles in liquids move more slowly.

Increasing the temperature makes diffusion occur faster.

Pressure In Gases

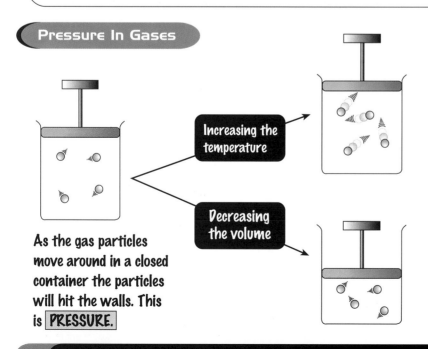

As the gas particles move around in a closed container the particles will hit the walls. This is PRESSURE.

If the TEMPERATURE IS INCREASED ...
... the particles move faster, ...
... hit the walls more often ...
... and the PRESSURE INCREASES.

If the VOLUME IS MADE SMALLER ...
... the distance between the walls is less, ...
... the particles hit the walls more often ...
... and the PRESSURE INCREASES.

If salt (sodium chloride) is put into water it will soon "disappear." This is called DISSOLVING.

The SUBSTANCE THAT DISSOLVES is called the SOLUTE e.g. sodium chloride.
The SUBSTANCE THAT DOES THE DISSOLVING is called the SOLVENT e.g. water.
The mixture of the SOLUTE AND SOLVENT is called the SOLUTION e.g. salt water.

An explanation of dissolving using the kinetic theory ...

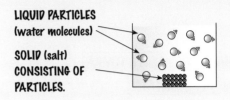

LIQUID PARTICLES
(water molecules)

SOLID (salt)
CONSISTING OF
PARTICLES.

The water particles move around and bump into the salt particles. The WATER AND SALT PARTICLES ARE ATTRACTED TO EACH OTHER.

SOME DISSOLVING
AND MIXING HAS
TAKEN PLACE.

WATER PARTICLES SURROUND THE SALT PARTICLES and the SOLID STRUCTURE BREAKS DOWN.

SOLID COMPLETELY
DISSOLVED AND
PARTICLES COMPLETELY
MIXED TOGETHER.

The SMALL SALT PARTICLES FIT IN BETWEEN THE WATER PARTICLES and are spread throughout the water.

Insoluble Substances

INSOLUBLE SUBSTANCES are ones that WILL NOT DISSOLVE.

Filtration

Insoluble substances can be separated from water by FILTERING.
e.g. sand and water.

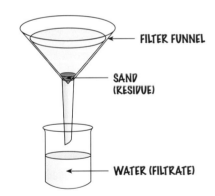

FILTER FUNNEL

SAND
(RESIDUE)

WATER (FILTRATE)

Not all substances dissolve in water, some are INSOLUBLE.

• Sand particles are TOO BIG to fit in between the water particles and they will NOT dissolve.

Water molecule

Large sand grains are too big to fit into the small spaces between the water molecule

• The attractions between calcium carbonate and water particles is not as great as the attraction between water particles, therefore ...
... calcium carbonate does not dissolve.

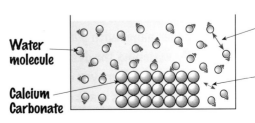

Water molecule

Calcium Carbonate

Attraction between water particles ...
... IS GREATER THAN ...
the attraction between water molecules and the calcium carbonate.

Crystallisation

CRYSTALLISATION can be used to SEPARATE A SOLUTE FROM THE SOLVENT in a solution.
ONLY the SOLUTE REMAINS at the end of the process.

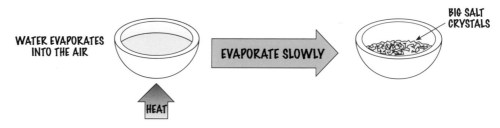

WATER EVAPORATES INTO THE AIR

EVAPORATE SLOWLY

BIG SALT CRYSTALS

HEAT

- If the SOLVENT EVAPORATES, SLOWLY then LARGE, WELL SHAPED CRYSTALS FORM.
- If the SOLVENT EVAPORATES RAPIDLY the crystals formed are VERY SMALL.

Distillation

DISTILLATION can be used to SEPARATE THE SOLVENT FROM THE SOLUTE in a solution.
The solvent is EVAPORATED and then CONDENSED.

THERMOMETER bulb opposite the outlet to the condenser ...
... measures the temperature of the gas leaving the round bottomed flask.

ANTIBUMP GRANULES stop large gas bubbles forming which cause the apparatus to "shudder" (bump).

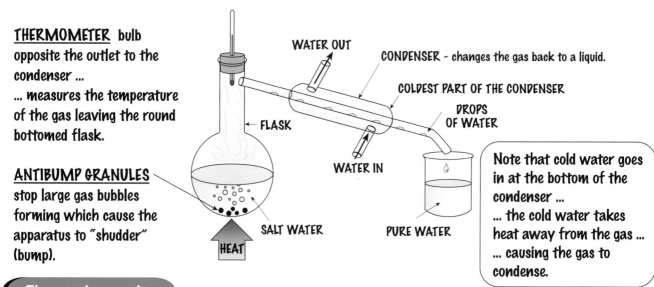

WATER OUT

CONDENSER - changes the gas back to a liquid.

COLDEST PART OF THE CONDENSER

DROPS OF WATER

FLASK

WATER IN

SALT WATER

HEAT

PURE WATER

Note that cold water goes in at the bottom of the condenser ...
... the cold water takes heat away from the gas ...
... causing the gas to condense.

Chromatography

CHROMATOGRAPHY can be used to SEPARATE OUT A MIXTURE OF DYES.
The dyes must have differing levels of solubility in the solvent.
The bottom of the paper is dipped in the solvent ...
... the solvent soaks up the paper ...
... the dyes that dissolve the best move further up the paper.

SEPARATED SOLIDS (showing that the original ink spot contained two different pigments)

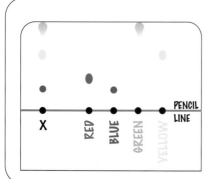

X   RED   BLUE   GREEN   YELLOW   PENCIL LINE

A chromatogram can be used to find out the dyes in a particular ink. The ink is put on a piece of paper along with pure colours. By matching the dyes in X with the pure colours you can find out what ink X is made of.

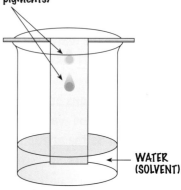

WATER (SOLVENT)

States Of Matter

- The three states of matter are solids, liquids and gases.
- Solids have a fixed volume and shape and do not flow.
- Liquids have a fixed volume but can change shape and flow.
- Gases have no fixed volume, can change shape, flow and be compressed.

- If a substance is heated it can change state.
- Even when being heated the temperature of a substance stays the same when it is changing state.
- When a substance is changing state energy is needed to overcome the forces of attraction between particles and to increase the particle's kinetic energy.

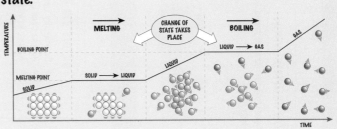

Kinetic Theory

- Diffusion is the mixing together of particles from two different liquids or gases.
- Diffusion occurs because the particles in liquids and gases can move.
- Diffusion happens much faster in gases than in liquids.

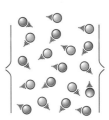

- When particles in a gas hit the side of a container they exert a pressure.
- If the temperature of a gas is increased or the volume of the container is made smaller then the pressure will increase.

- Substances dissolve in water because the water particles surround the solute and break down the solid structure.

HIGHER/SPECIAL TIER

- Substances that are insoluble are either made up of large particles or the force of attraction between the water and solute particles is not as great as the attraction between water particles.

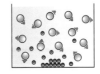

- Crystallisation can separate a solute from the solvent in a solution.
- Distillation can separate a solvent from the solute in a solution.
- Chromatography can separate out different coloured dyes in an ink.

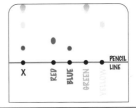

Record the SEVEN 'States of Matter' and TEN 'Kinetic Theory' facts on your tape.
Now - READ, COVER WRITE and CHECK the SEVENTEEN facts.

Atomic Structure

SUB-ATOMIC PARTICLES

Particles	Relative Mass	Relative Charge
Proton	1	+1
Neutron	1	0
Electron	$1/1840$	-1

MASS NUMBER & ATOMIC NUMBER

Mass Number 19

Atomic (Proton) 9
Number

Mass Number = No. of Protons and Neutrons

Atomic Number = No. of Protons

ELECTRON CONFIGURATION

- Shows how electrons are arranged in their energy levels.

$^{14}_{7}N$ (2,5)

ISOTOPES

- Same number of protons but different number of neutrons
- Same chemical reactions

$^{35}_{17}Cl$ $^{37}_{17}Cl$

The Periodic Table

HISTORY OF THE PERIODIC TABLE

- NEWLANDS - arranged elements in order of relative atomic mass.

Li Be B C N O F Na Mg Al

- MENDELEEV - left gaps for undiscovered elements and changed the order of elements to "group" elements with similar chemical properties

GROUP VIII - THE NOBLE GASES

- Chemically unreactive due to full outer energy levels.
- Helium used in airships.
- Argon, krypton and neon used in lighting.

GROUP VII - THE HALOGENS

- Elements have coloured vapours and are made up of diatomic molecules.
- All have seven electrons in their outermost energy level.
- More reactive halogens will displace a less reactive halogen from its compound.
- Decrease in reactivity going down the group.

Bromine molecules

GROUP I - THE ALKALI METALS

- All have one electron in their outermost energy level.
- React with water to produce hydroxides and hydrogen gas.
- Have characteristic colours in a flame test.
- Increase in reactivity going down the group.

Li Na K

TRANSITION METALS

- Tend to be hard, strong and with high melting and boiling points.
- Have coloured compounds.
- Carbonates tend to decompose on heating.
- Sodium Hydroxide can be used to test for Cu^{2+}, Fe^{2+} and Fe^{3+}.

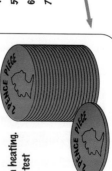

Structure Of An Atom

Everything is made up of atoms.

Atoms contain three types of particles: protons, neutrons (except hydrogen!) and electrons.

This is an atom of fluorine:

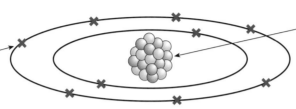

The electrons ✗ move around the nucleus in energy levels or orbitals.

This is the nucleus it contains the protons ⚪ which are positively charged and neutrons ⚪ which are neutral. The nucleus is small and heavy.

ATOMIC PARTICLE		RELATIVE MASS	RELATIVE CHARGE
PROTON	⚪	1	+1
NEUTRON	⚪	1	0
ELECTRON	✗	1/1840 (almost nothing)	-1

Mass Number And Atomic Number

You will find in the Periodic Table each element's symbol has two numbers by it.
Imagine there is an element X.

MASS NUMBER is the total number of protons and neutrons in the atom.

ATOMIC NUMBER is the number of protons in the atom. Also called the Proton Number.

$$_Z^A X$$

← symbol of the element

The ATOMIC NUMBER gives ...the NUMBER OF PROTONS which is equal to the NUMBER OF ELECTRONS...
... because atoms have no overall charge.

NUMBER OF NEUTRONS = MASS NUMBER - ATOMIC NUMBER

EXAMPLES:

$_1^1 H$
HYDROGEN
1 proton
1 electron
0 neutrons (1-1)

$_8^{16} O$
OXYGEN
8 protons
8 electrons
8 neutrons (16-8)

$_9^{19} F$
FLUORINE
9 protons
9 electrons
10 neutrons (19-9)

$_{11}^{23} Na$
SODIUM
11 protons
11 electrons
12 neutrons (23-11)

- The electron configuration shows how electrons are arranged in the energy levels.
- This is very important when trying to explain how elements react.
- The first energy level (nearest the nucleus) can hold up to two electrons before it is full …
    … the second can hold up to eight electrons and …
    … the third can hold up to eight electrons.

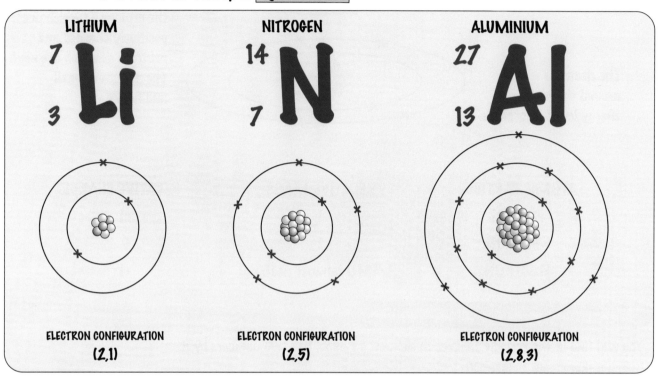

LITHIUM	NITROGEN	ALUMINIUM
ELECTRON CONFIGURATION (2,1)	ELECTRON CONFIGURATION (2,5)	ELECTRON CONFIGURATION (2,8,3)

Isotopes

ALL ATOMS of a particular ELEMENT have the SAME NUMBER OF PROTONS.
The NUMBER of PROTONS, DEFINES THE ELEMENT.
However some atoms of the SAME ELEMENT can have DIFFERENT NUMBERS OF NEUTRONS …
… these are called ISOTOPES.
They are easy to spot because they have the SAME ATOMIC NUMBER but a DIFFERENT MASS NUMBER.

FOR EXAMPLE: CHLORINE …

$^{35}_{17}Cl$ 17 protons
17 electrons
18 neutrons (35-17)

$^{37}_{17}Cl$ 17 protons
17 electrons
20 neutrons (37-17)

FOR EXAMPLE: CARBON …

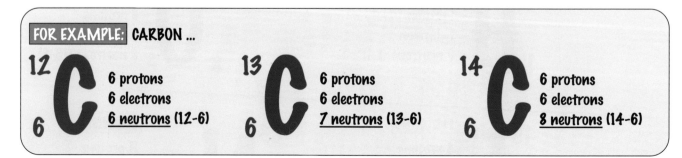

$^{12}_{6}C$ 6 protons
6 electrons
6 neutrons (12-6)

$^{13}_{6}C$ 6 protons
6 electrons
7 neutrons (13-6)

$^{14}_{6}C$ 6 protons
6 electrons
8 neutrons (14-6)

- Remember, in an isotope the number of neutrons differ …
    … but because the isotopes of an element have the same electron configuration their reactions are the same.

JOHN NEWLANDS (1864)

- Arranged the <u>63</u> elements in order of their RELATIVE ATOMIC MASS ...

  ... he noticed that every eighth element had similar chemical properties

  (a similar element appeared PERIODICALLY) ...

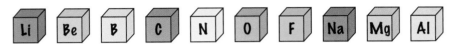

...unfortunately because there were many elements missing his periodic pattern soon disappeared!!

DIMITRI MENDELEEV (1869)

- Used Newlands ideas but importantly LEFT GAPS for the undiscovered elements ...

  ... and was prepared to swap around some of the elements so that they were "grouped" together with other elements that had similar chemical properties.

- Mendeleev predicted the properties of some undiscovered elements using his Periodic table ...

  ... his predictions were right!

- Mendeleev's Periodic table forms the basis of the Modern Periodic Table.

The Modern Periodic Table

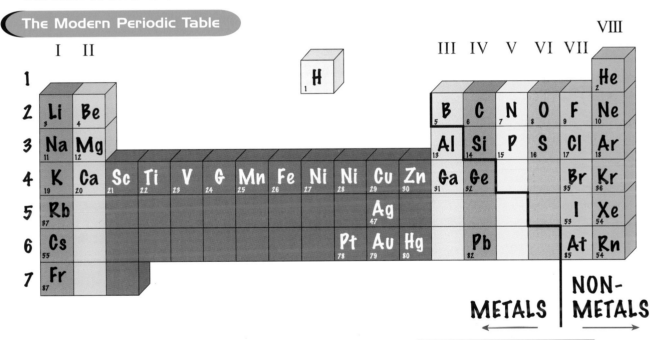

- The 90 naturally occurring elements are arranged in order of their ATOMIC (PROTON) NUMBER

- The atoms in a single element are identical.

- The atoms of each element are different to the atoms of the other elements.

Vertical rows are called GROUPS.
Elements in a particular group have
SIMILAR CHEMICAL PROPERTIES since they
have the same number of electrons in their
outermost energy level ...
... e.g. elements in Group I have one electron,
elements in Group II have two electrons ...
and so on.

Horizontal rows are called PERIODS.
The CHEMICAL PROPERTIES of the elements
GRADUALLY CHANGE across each period.
This is because the number of electrons in the atoms'
outermost energy level gradually changes across
the period.

All the elements in GROUP I have ONE ELECTRON in their outermost energy level. The elements all have similar chemical reactions.

The ALKALI METALS are stored under oils because they react very vigorously with water.

If lithium, sodium or potassium are put in cold water ...

... they FLOAT ON TOP because of their LOW DENSITY and ...

... MELT because the heat from the reaction is great enough to turn them into liquids. Alkali metals have LOW MELTING POINTS.

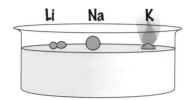

When alkali metals react with water a METAL HYDROXIDE and HYDROGEN GAS are formed.

The metal hydroxide (eg. lithium hydroxide, sodium hydroxide) dissolves in water to form an ALKALINE SOLUTION.

Flame Tests

Lithium, sodium and potassium compounds can be recognised by their colours in a flame test.

The wire is cleaned in acid before being dipped into the compound and then put into the bunsen flame.

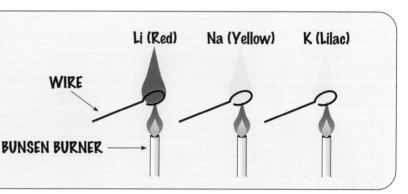

WIRE

BUNSEN BURNER

Trends In Group I

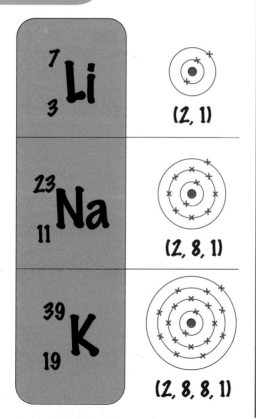

LOWER MELTING AND BOILING POINTS

REACTIVITY INCREASES

$^{7}_{3}$ Li

(2, 1)

$^{23}_{11}$ Na

(2, 8, 1)

$^{39}_{19}$ K

(2, 8, 8, 1)

HIGHER TIER

Reactivity in Group I

• The FURTHER DOWN GROUP I the metal is the GREATER ITS REACTIVITY because ... ... during reactions Group I metals LOSE one electron to form an ion with a +1 charge.

• The metal MORE EASILY LOSES ITS ELECTRON from the outermost energy level as:

❶ The atomic radius increases (the distance from the positive nucleus to the outermost energy level).

❷ The number of energy levels that "shield" the electron in the outermost energy level from the attraction of the positive nucleus increases.

The TRANSITION METALS include all the elements between Group II and Group III in the Periodic Table.

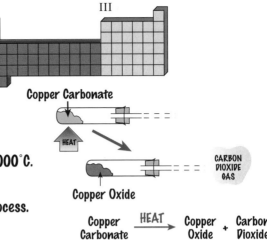

Properties Of The Transition Metals

- Transition metal compounds are often coloured.
- Transition metals are hard and mechanically strong.
- Transition metals have high melting and boiling points e.g. iron, copper and titanium all have melting points over 1000°C.
- Carbonates of transition metals breakdown when heated giving off carbon dioxide and changing colour during the process.

Copper Carbonate

HEAT

Copper Oxide

CARBON DIOXIDE GAS

$$Copper\ Carbonate \xrightarrow{HEAT} Copper\ Oxide + Carbon\ Dioxide$$

Uses Of The Transition Metals

- Transition metals are often catalysts e.g. Iron is used in the Haber Process.
- Copper, Tin and Zinc can be used to make coins - they are hard-wearing.
- Copper is used in electrical wiring because it is a good conductor ...
  ... and to make hot water pipes because it does not corrode.

Identifying Copper$_{(II)}$, Iron$_{(II)}$ and Iron$_{(III)}$ Ions

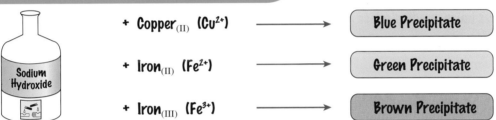

Sodium Hydroxide

- $+$ Copper$_{(II)}$ (Cu^{2+}) $\longrightarrow$ **Blue Precipitate**
- $+$ Iron$_{(II)}$ (Fe^{2+}) $\longrightarrow$ **Green Precipitate**
- $+$ Iron$_{(III)}$ (Fe^{3+}) $\longrightarrow$ **Brown Precipitate**

HIGHER TIER

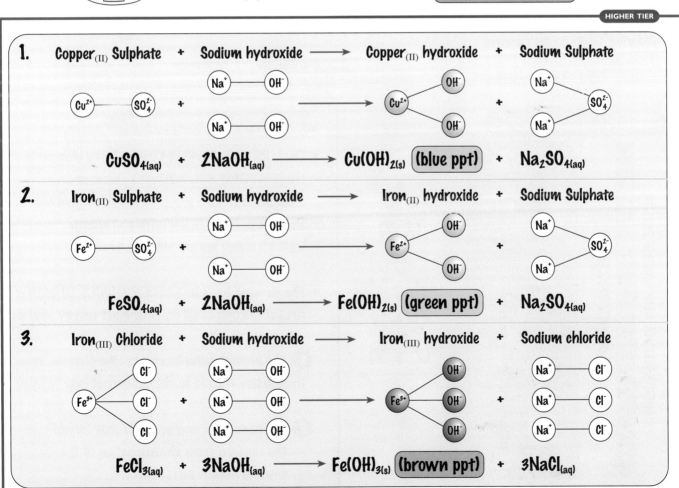

1. Copper$_{(II)}$ Sulphate + Sodium hydroxide $\longrightarrow$ Copper$_{(II)}$ hydroxide + Sodium Sulphate

$$CuSO_{4(aq)} + 2NaOH_{(aq)} \longrightarrow Cu(OH)_{2(s)}\ \text{(blue ppt)} + Na_2SO_{4(aq)}$$

2. Iron$_{(II)}$ Sulphate + Sodium hydroxide $\longrightarrow$ Iron$_{(II)}$ hydroxide + Sodium Sulphate

$$FeSO_{4(aq)} + 2NaOH_{(aq)} \longrightarrow Fe(OH)_{2(s)}\ \text{(green ppt)} + Na_2SO_{4(aq)}$$

3. Iron$_{(III)}$ Chloride + Sodium hydroxide $\longrightarrow$ Iron$_{(III)}$ hydroxide + Sodium chloride

$$FeCl_{3(aq)} + 3NaOH_{(aq)} \longrightarrow Fe(OH)_{3(s)}\ \text{(brown ppt)} + 3NaCl_{(aq)}$$

All the elements in GROUP VII have SEVEN electrons in their outermost energy level.
The HALOGENS all have similar chemical reactions.

Properties of the Halogens

- The halogens are all non-metals and have coloured vapours.
- The element of the halogens are diatomic, ...
  ... this means two atoms join together to make a molecule F_2, Cl_2, Br_2, I_2
- They can react with both metals and other non-metals.

Bromine Molecules

CHLORINE   BROMINE   IODINE

Uses of the Halogens

- Iodine solution is used as an antiseptic.
- Chlorine (See P44 for uses).
- Bromine will react with silver to form silver bromide.
  Silver bromide changes colour when light shines on it ...
  ... and is used to make photographic film.

Iodine Solution

Film 400

Displacement Reactions

A more reactive halogen will displace a less reactive halogen from its compound.

Chlorine gas ⟶

Bromine being formed due to the displacement reaction

Potassium Bromide solution

Chlorine   - Most reactive
Bromine
Iodine   - Least reactive

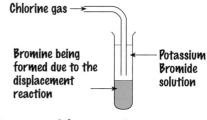

	Potassium Chloride $KCl_{(aq)}$	Potassium Bromide $KBr_{(aq)}$	Potassium Iodide $KI_{(aq)}$
Chlorine Cl_2	✕	+ KCl Bromine	+ KCl Iodine
Bromine Br_2	No Reaction	✕	+ KBr Iodine
Iodine I_2	No Reaction	No Reaction	✕

Trends In Group VII

HIGHER MELTING AND BOILING POINTS

REACTIVITY DECREASES

19 F 9

(2, 7)

35 Cl 17

(2, 8, 7)

80 Br 35

HIGHER TIER

Reactivity in Group VII

- The FURTHER DOWN GROUP VII the element is the LOWER IT'S REACTIVITY because ...
  ... during reactions Group VII elements gain one electron to form an ion with a -1 charge (called a halide ion e.g. chloride, bromide).

- The element finds it MORE DIFFICULT TO GAIN AN ELECTRON to fill its outermost energy level as:

  ❶ The atomic radius increases (the distance from the positive nucleus to the outermost energy level).

  ❷ The number of energy levels that "shield" the electron from the attraction of the positive nucleus increases.

The elements in Group VIII are all quite unreactive ...
... and are called the NOBLE GASES.

VIII

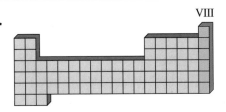

Properties Of The Noble Gases

- They have LOW melting and boiling points.
- They are made up of SINGLE ATOMS.

Helium Atoms (monatomic)

Uses Of The Noble Gases

- Helium is used in airships because it is much less dense than air.

- Argon is used in light bulbs because it is unreactive and provides an inert atmosphere.

- Argon, Krypton and Neon are all used in filament lamps and discharge tubes.

Trends In Group VIII

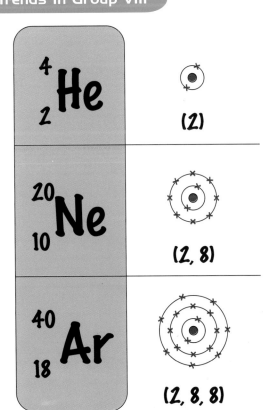

$^{4}_{2}$He   (2)

$^{20}_{10}$Ne   (2, 8)

$^{40}_{18}$Ar   (2, 8, 8)

HIGHER TIER

Reactivity in Group VIII

- The Noble Gases all have ...
  ... FULL OUTERMOST ENERGY LEVELS ...
  ... they DO NOT need to lose or gain electrons in reactions to become stable and ...
  ... so they do not react with many other elements.

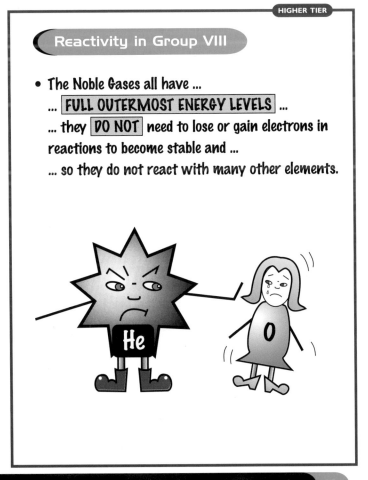

Atomic Structure

- Atoms are made up from protons, electrons and neutrons.
- Two electrons fit in the first energy level before it is full but the second and third energy levels can both hold up to eight electrons.
- Isotopes are atoms of an element that have the same atomic (proton) number but a different mass number.
- Isotopes of an element have the same chemical reactions because their electron configuration is identical.

The Periodic Table

HISTORY OF THE PERIODIC TABLE

- Originally Newlands arranged the elements in order of relative atomic mass.
- Mendeleev - left gaps for undiscovered elements and grouped together elements with similar properties.
- Today the periodic table contains elements arranged in order of atomic (proton) number.
- Groups contain elements with similar chemical properties and the same number of electrons in their outermost energy level e.g. Group I = one electron, Group II = two electrons ... and so on.

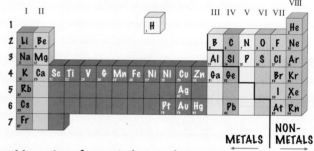

THE ALKALI METALS (GROUP I)

- React vigorously with water to produce a metal hydroxide and hydrogen gas.
- Have characteristic flames - Li (Red), Na (Yellow), K (Lilac).
- Increase in reactivity going down the group.

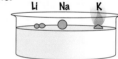

THE TRANSITION METALS

- Have high melting and boiling points, are hard and strong with coloured compounds.
- Can be identified by reacting with sodium hydroxide – Cu^{2+} (blue), Fe^{2+} (green) and Fe^{3+} (brown).

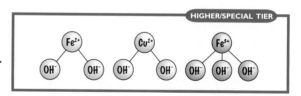

HIGHER/SPECIAL TIER

THE HALOGENS (GROUP VII)

- Have coloured vapours and diatomic molecules.
- A more reactive halogen will displace a less reactive halogen from its compound.
- Decrease in reactivity going down the group.

THE NOBLE GASES (GROUP VIII)

- Are chemically unreactive due to their full outermost energy levels.
- Can be used in airships (helium) or lighting (neon, argon and krypton).

Record the FOUR 'Atomic Structure' and FOURTEEN 'Periodic Table' facts on your tape.

Now - READ, COVER, WRITE and CHECK the EIGHTEEN facts.

Bonding

COVALENT BONDING - GIANT MOLECULES

- Giant molecules have very strong covalent bonds throughout the whole structure.
- Giant molecules have very high melting and boiling points.

HIGHER/SPECIAL TIER

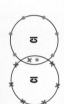

COVALENT BONDING - SIMPLE MOLECULES

- Covalent bonds are formed by sharing electrons.

Cl Cl

- Simple molecules have a low melting and boiling point, do not dissolve in water or conduct electricity.

IONIC BONDING

- Metals donate electrons to non-metals.

Na Cl

ELECTRON

- Positive and negative ions are formed.
- Ionic substances have high melting points, dissolve in water and conduct electricity when molten or dissolved in water.

ELECTROLYSIS

Heat

- Positive ions that can move are attracted to the negative cathode.
- Negative ions that can move are attracted to the positive anode.

HIGHER/SPECIAL TIER

- At the Cathode positive ions gain electrons.

$$Zn^{2+} + 2e^- \rightarrow Zn$$

- At the Anode negative ions give up electrons.

$$2Br^- - 2e^- \rightarrow Br_2$$

Equation Writing

Percentage

$$Percentage = \frac{Mass\ of\ element\ \times 100}{M_r\ of\ compound}$$

M_r

- Relative formula mass is the sum of the A_r's of each element in the substance formula.

REACTANTS ➔ PRODUCTS

A_r

- Relative atomic mass of an element (compared to carbon -12).

REACTING MASSES

- Total mass of reactants = Total mass of products

- Divide masses by A_r of the element
- Simplify the ratios
- Write the formula

SIMPLEST FORMULA

EMPIRICAL FORMULA

VOLUME OF GASES IN A REACTION

- Relative formula mass of gas in grams occupies 24 litres at RTP.

- Write down the equation and work out M_r of each substance.
- Check total mass of reactants = Total mass of products
- Apply ratios and then convert mass to volume of gas.

WRITING FORMULA

Mg^{2+} (two positive charges)

$Cl-Cl-$ (two negative charges)

➔ $Mg\,Cl_2$

WRITING FULLY BALANCED EQUATIONS

HIGHER/SPECIAL TIER

- 1. Write a word equation.
- 2. Write down the formulae.
- 3. Balance the equation.
- 4. Write down the state symbol (s), (l), (g) or (aq)

1 2 3 4

In a chemical reaction ATOMS will try to become more CHEMICALLY STABLE ...
... by filling or emptying their OUTERMOST ENERGY LEVELS ...
... BY GAINING or LOSING ELECTRONS.

NON-METALS can either GAIN ELECTRONS FROM METALS or SHARE ELECTRONS with other non-metals.

The SHARING OF ELECTRONS forms a COVALENT BOND.

CHLORINE ATOMS (only outermost energy levels shown) ...

Shared pair
of electrons

  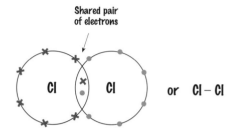

or   Cl – Cl

... the atoms BOTH need to gain an electron
to fill their outermost energy levels ...

... they achieve this by sharing one pair
of electrons in a COVALENT BOND.

The covalent bond BETWEEN the two
ATOMS is VERY STRONG but the
attraction between MOLECULES is WEAK.
This means simple molecules have low melting
and boiling points ...
... do not dissolve in water ...
... and have no overall electric charge so they
CANNOT conduct electricity.

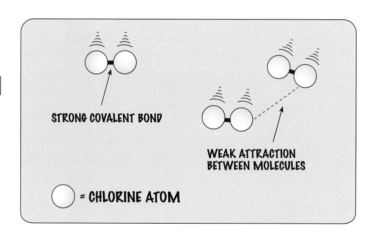

STRONG COVALENT BOND

WEAK ATTRACTION
BETWEEN MOLECULES

○ = CHLORINE ATOM

Other Examples Include   (Outermost shells only)

Water

H – O – H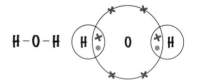

Hydrogen

H – H

Methane

H
|
H – C – H
|
H

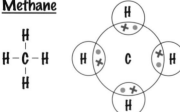

Oxygen

O = O   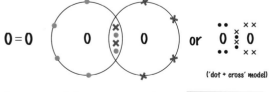   or

('dot + cross' model)

(two pairs of shared electrons form a DOUBLE BOND)

Ammonia

H – N – H
|
H

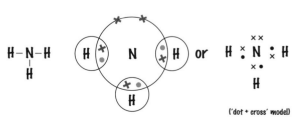   or

('dot + cross' model)

In giant molecules electrons are shared by the atoms throughout a large regular structure <u>CALLED A LATTICE</u>.

These strong covalent bonds throughout the giant lattice means the substances have high melting and boiling points.

As the giant molecules have no overall electric charge they do not conduct electricity or dissolve in water.

Firing Clay

Wet clay contains layers of silicate ...
... with water molecules in between ...
... that allow the layers to slide over each other.

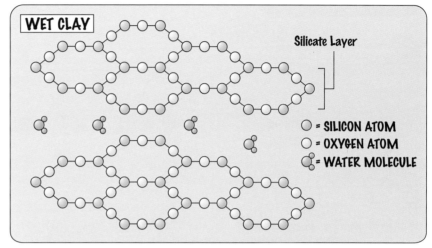

WET CLAY

Silicate Layer

◉ = SILICON ATOM
○ = OXYGEN ATOM
❀ = WATER MOLECULE

When clay is fired (heated in a Kiln) ...
... the water between the layers is driven off ...
... and new strong bonds link the silicate layers together.

The new material formed is very hard ...
... and fired clays are called ceramics.

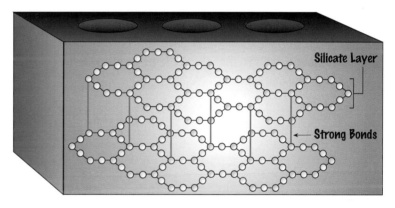

Silicate Layer

← Strong Bonds

HIGHER/SPECIAL TIER

Diamond (A Form Of Carbon)

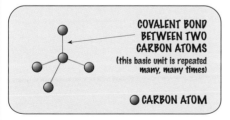

COVALENT BOND BETWEEN TWO CARBON ATOMS
(this basic unit is repeated many, many times)

● CARBON ATOM

- A GIANT, RIGID COVALENT STRUCTURE (LATTICE) where EACH CARBON ATOM ...
- ... forms FOUR COVALENT BONDS with OTHER CARBON ATOMS.
- The LARGE NUMBER of COVALENT BONDS results in diamond having a <u>VERY HIGH MELTING POINT</u> and being <u>VERY HARD</u>.

Graphite (A Form Of Carbon)

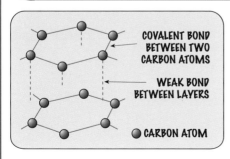

COVALENT BOND BETWEEN TWO CARBON ATOMS

WEAK BOND BETWEEN LAYERS

● CARBON ATOM

- A GIANT, COVALENT STRUCTURE (LATTICE) in which EACH CARBON ATOM ...
- ... forms THREE COVALENT BONDS with OTHER CARBON ATOMS.
- This leaves a FREE ELECTRON and so graphite <u>CONDUCTS ELECTRICITY</u>.
- It has LAYERS which can SLIDE PAST EACH OTHER BECAUSE ...
- ... between LAYERS there are WEAK FORCES of ATTRACTION ...
- ... and so graphite can be used as a LUBRICANT.

To become chemically stable a metal atom must empty its outermost energy level ...

... by donating (giving) an electron or electrons ...

... to a non-metal which uses the electron(s) to fill its outermost energy level.

The particles formed during this bonding have an overall electrical charge and are called IONS.

Sodium Chloride

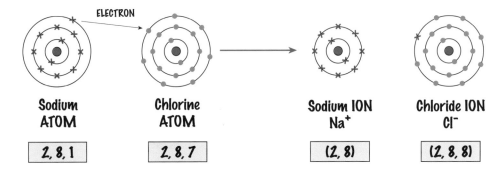

| Sodium ATOM | Chlorine ATOM | Sodium ION Na^+ | Chloride ION Cl^- |
| 2, 8, 1 | 2, 8, 7 | (2, 8) | (2, 8, 8) |

The sodium atom donates the ONE electron from its outermost energy level ...

... to the chlorine atom which already has SEVEN electrons in its outermost energy level ...

... so that they BOTH HAVE FULL OUTERMOST ENERGY LEVELS and are chemically stable.

The sodium atom now has one less electron and becomes a positively charged SODIUM ION - Na⁺ ...

... whereas the chlorine atom has gained an electron and becomes a negatively charged CHLORIDE ION - Cl⁻.

Magnesium Oxide

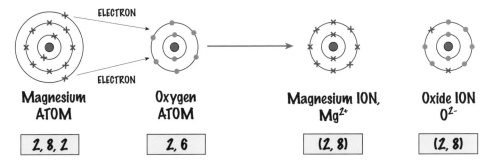

| Magnesium ATOM | Oxygen ATOM | Magnesium ION, Mg^{2+} | Oxide ION O^{2-} |
| 2, 8, 2 | 2, 6 | (2, 8) | (2, 8) |

The magnesium atom donates the TWO electrons from its outermost energy level ...

... to the oxygen atom which already has SIX electrons in its outermost energy level ...

... so that they BOTH HAVE FULL OUTERMOST ENERGY LEVELS and are chemically stable.

Properties Of Ionic Solids

Ionic solids, like sodium chloride, consists of a lattice held together by the forces of attraction between POSITIVE sodium ions (+) and NEGATIVE chloride ions (-).

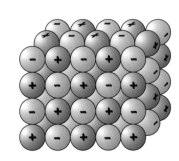

IONIC SOLIDS

• Have high melting and boiling points ...

• ... dissolve in water due to the strong bonds formed between the molecules ...

• ... and will conduct electricity when MOLTEN OR DISSOLVED in water because the ions are free to move.

When electricity is passed through a molten ionic substance ...
... or one that has been dissolved in water the ionic substance is broken down.
This is called ELECTROLYSIS.

Electrolysis Of Molten Zinc Bromide

When zinc bromide is heated ...
... the ionic lattice breaks down ...
... to give zinc and bromide ions ...
...which are free to move.

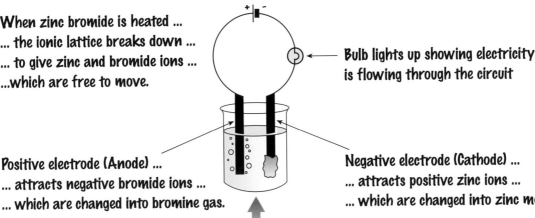

Bulb lights up showing electricity is flowing through the circuit

Positive electrode (Anode) ...
... attracts negative bromide ions ...
... which are changed into bromine gas.

Negative electrode (Cathode) ...
... attracts positive zinc ions ...
... which are changed into zinc metal.

Heat

HIGHER/SPECIAL TIER

Explaining The Electrolysis Of Zinc Bromide

AT THE ANODE
Mobile bromide ions are attracted
to the positive anode ...
... where they give up electrons ...
... to form bromine atoms.
Two bromine atoms link
to form a molecule

$$2Br^-_{(l)} - 2e^- \longrightarrow Br_{2(g)}$$

Loss of electrons is called OXIDATION.

AT THE CATHODE
Mobile zinc ions are attracted
to the negative cathode ...
... where they gain electrons ...
... to form zinc atoms.

$$Zn^{2+}_{(l)} + 2e^- \longrightarrow Zn_{(l)}$$

Gain of electrons is called REDUCTION.

Electrolysis Of Water

Small amounts of acid are added
to the water to make it conduct
electricity better.

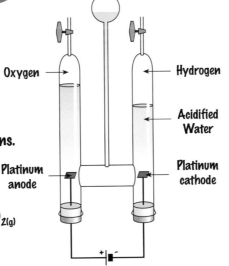

Oxygen

Hydrogen

Acidified Water

AT THE ANODE
Hydroxide ions (OH⁻) move to the
positive anode and give up electrons.

Platinum anode

Platinum cathode

$$4OH^-_{(aq)} + 4e^- \longrightarrow 2H_2O_{(l)} + O_{2(g)}$$

AT THE CATHODE
Hydrogen ions (H⁺) move
to the negative cathode
and gain electrons.

$$4H^+_{(aq)} + 4e^- \longrightarrow 2H_{2(g)}$$

Note twice as much hydrogen
is produced as oxygen.

Battery

- Before you can start writing formula on your own it is important that you understand what formula show.
- Chemist use formula to show ...
- ... the different elements and ...
- ... the number of particles of each element in a substance.

e.g.

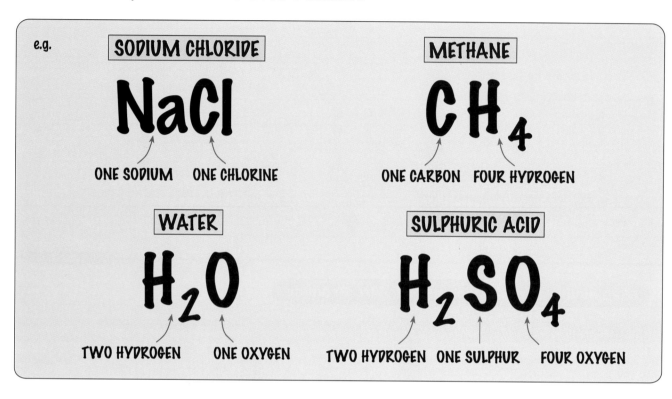

SODIUM CHLORIDE

$NaCl$

ONE SODIUM   ONE CHLORINE

METHANE

CH_4

ONE CARBON   FOUR HYDROGEN

WATER

H_2O

TWO HYDROGEN   ONE OXYGEN

SULPHURIC ACID

H_2SO_4

TWO HYDROGEN   ONE SULPHUR   FOUR OXYGEN

If brackets are put around part of the formula remember to multiply everything inside the bracket by the number outside.

e.g.

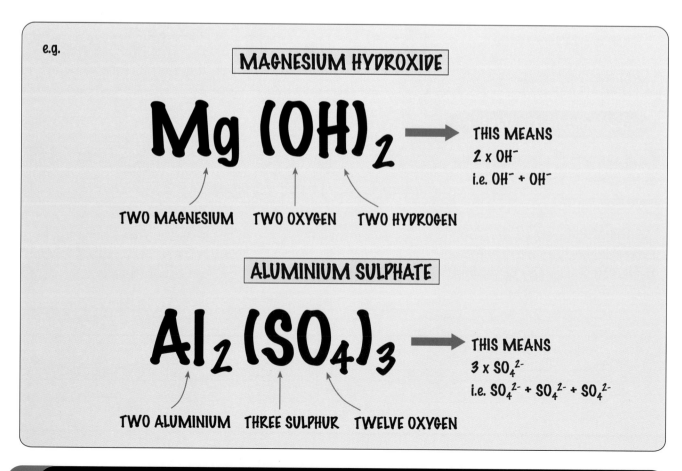

MAGNESIUM HYDROXIDE

$Mg(OH)_2$ ➞ THIS MEANS
$2 \times OH^-$
i.e. $OH^- + OH^-$

TWO MAGNESIUM   TWO OXYGEN   TWO HYDROGEN

ALUMINIUM SULPHATE

$Al_2(SO_4)_3$ ➞ THIS MEANS
$3 \times SO_4^{2-}$
i.e. $SO_4^{2-} + SO_4^{2-} + SO_4^{2-}$

TWO ALUMINIUM   THREE SULPHUR   TWELVE OXYGEN

Writing Your Own Formula

- To work out a formula you must have the correct number of positive and negative ions ...
  ... so that OVERALL there is no charge.

It is probably worth remembering some well used formula.

Water - H_2O

Carbon Dioxide - CO_2

Oxygen - O_2

Sulphuric Acid - H_2SO_4

Hydrochloric Acid - HCl

Nitric Acid - HNO_3

POSITIVE IONS		NEGATIVE IONS	
H^+	Hydrogen	Cl^-	Chloride
Na^+	Sodium	Br^-	Bromide
K^+	Potassium	F^-	Fluoride
Li^+	Lithium	I^-	Iodide
Ca^{2+}	Calcium	O^{2-}	Oxide
Mg^{2+}	Magnesium	*OH^-	Hydroxide
Cu^{2+}	Copper(II)	*NO_3^-	Nitrate ion
Fe^{2+}	Iron(II)	*SO_4^{2-}	Sulphate ion
Fe^{3+}	Iron(III)	*CO_3^{2-}	Carbonate ion
Zn^{2+}	Zinc		
Al^{3+}	Aluminium		

* If MORE THAN ONE of these ions are needed in the formula then brackets should be used.

e.g. SODIUM CHLORIDE

(one positive charge)   (one negative charge)   →   Na Cl

e.g. MAGNESIUM CHLORIDE

(two positive charges)   (two negative charges)   →   Mg Cl_2

e.g. ALUMINIUM OXIDE

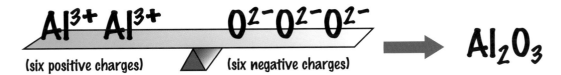

(six positive charges)   (six negative charges)   → Al_2O_3

e.g. IRON (III) HYDROXIDE

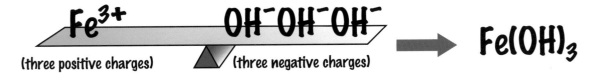

(three positive charges)   (three negative charges)   → $Fe(OH)_3$

Writing Word Equations

Chemists show what has happened during a reaction in a word equation ...

... with the substances reacting, the REACTANTS on one side of the equation ...

... and the new substances formed, the PRODUCTS on the other.

$$REACTANTS \longrightarrow PRODUCTS$$

There are many equations you need to know but learning some general rules can save time!

$$METAL + ACID \longrightarrow SALT + HYDROGEN$$

$$BASE/ALKALI + ACID \longrightarrow SALT + WATER$$

$$CARBONATE + ACID \longrightarrow SALT + CARBON\ DIOXIDE + WATER$$

To name the SALT write down the metal

✦ If sulphuric acid is used a SULPHATE is formed. e.g. Magnesium Sulphate

✦ If hydrochloric acid is used a CHLORIDE is formed. e.g. Copper Chloride

✦ If nitric acid is used a NITRATE is formed. e.g Sodium Nitrate

---

HIGHER/SPECIAL TIER

Writing Symbol Equations

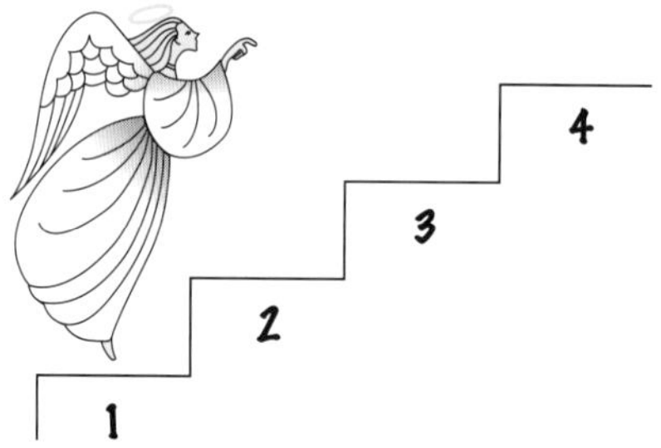

THERE ARE FOUR STEPS TO THE 'EQUATION WRITING HEAVEN'

① Write a word equation
e.g. Magnesium reacts with hydrochloric acid.

Magnesium + Hydrochloric Acid → Magnesium Chloride + Hydrogen

② Write down all the formula for the reactants and products
(remember hydrogen gas is DIATOMIC).

$$Mg + HCl \longrightarrow MgCl_2 + H_2$$

③ Balance the equation, you need the same number of each element on both the reactants and products side.
Only put NUMBERS IN FRONT of formulae.
Do not change formulae!

$$Mg + 2HCl \longrightarrow MgCl_2 + H_2$$

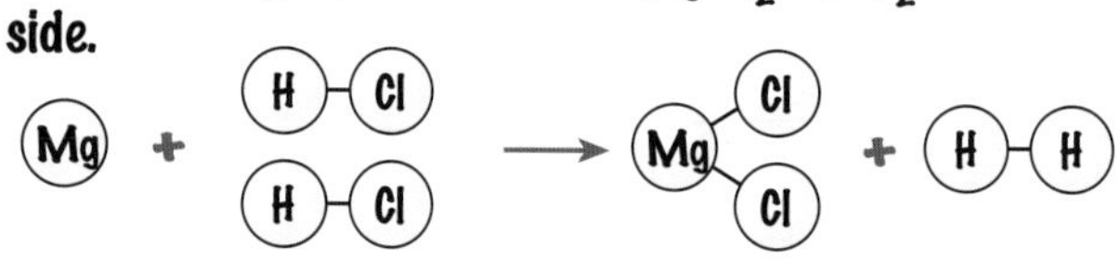

④ Add state symbols
s = solid, l = liquids, g = gases, aq = aqueous solution

$$Mg_{(s)} + 2HCl_{(aq)} \longrightarrow MgCl_{2(aq)} + H_{2(g)}$$

Relative Atomic Mass, A_r

Atoms are too small for their actual atomic mass to be of much use to us.

To make things more manageable we use RELATIVE ATOMIC MASS, A_r.

• Basically this is just the MASS OF A PARTICULAR ATOM ...

• ... compared to the MASS OF AN ATOM OF HYDROGEN, (the lightest atom of all.)

(In fact we now use 1/12th the mass of a CARBON ATOM, but it doesn't make any real difference!)

• You will be supplied with the A_r of elements ...

... in the examination question or data booklet.

A_r of Hydrogen atom	A_r of Carbon atom	A_r of Oxygen atom	A_r of Sodium atom	A_r of Magnesium atom	A_r of Sulphur atom	A_r of Potassium atom
1	12	16	23	24	32	39

• So, in the examples above Carbon is twelve times heavier than Hydrogen, but ...

... is only half as heavy as Magnesium, which is three quarters as heavy as Sulphur ...

... which is twice as heavy as Oxygen and so on, and so on ...

• We can use this idea to calculate the ⟨RELATIVE FORMULA MASS⟩ of compounds.

Relative Formula Mass, M_r

The relative formula mass of a compound is simply the relative atomic masses of all its elements added together. So in other words, if water has an M_r of 18, it is 18 times heavier than an atom of Hydrogen, or 1.5 times heavier than a Carbon atom! Get it?

• To calculate M_r, we need the FORMULA OF THE COMPOUND, and the A_r of ALL THE ATOMS INVOLVED.

EXAMPLE 1 Using the data above, find the M_r of Water, H_2O

STEP 1: the Formula ... H_2O

STEP 2: the A_r's ... $(2 \times 1) + 16$

STEP 3: the M_r ... $2 + 16 = \underline{18}$

EXAMPLE 2 Using the data above, find the M_r of Sodium Hydroxide, NaOH

STEP 1: the Formula ... NaOH

STEP 2: the A_r's ... $23 + 16 + 1$

STEP 3: the M_r ... $23 + 16 + 1 = \underline{40}$

EXAMPLE 3 Using the data above, find the M_r of Potassium Carbonate, K_2CO_3

STEP 1: the Formula ... K_2CO_3

STEP 2: the A_r's ... $(39 \times 2) + 12 + (16 \times 3)$

STEP 3: the M_r ... $78 + 12 + 48 = \underline{138}$

Working Out Percentages

If 12 pupils in a class of 30 are left handed, you could work out the percentage of left handers in the following way ...

$$\frac{\text{No. OF LEFT HANDERS}}{\text{TOTAL No. IN CLASS}} \times 100$$, ... in this case $\frac{12}{30} \times 100 = \underline{40.0\%}$

You use exactly the same principle in calculating percentage mass of an element in a compound, except this time we express it as ...

$$\frac{\text{MASS OF ELEMENT IN THE COMPOUND}}{\text{RELATIVE FORMULA MASS OF COMPOUND } (M_r)} \times 100$$ The mass of the compound is the relative formula mass.

- All you need to know is the FORMULA OF THE COMPOUND and the RELATIVE ATOMIC MASS of all the atoms.

Examples Of Percentage Mass Questions

EXAMPLE 1 "Calculate the percentage mass of Magnesium in Magnesium Oxide, MgO."

MASS OF MAGNESIUM = 24 (since this is its A_r, and there's only one atom of it!).

RELATIVE FORMULA MASS (M_r) of MgO = (A_r for Mg) 24 + (A_r for O) 16 = 40.

Substituting into our formula ... $\dfrac{\text{MASS OF ELEMENT}}{M_r \text{ OF COMPOUND}} \times 100$, ... we get $\frac{24}{40} \times 100 = \underline{60.0\%}$

EXAMPLE 2 "Calculate the percentage mass of Oxygen in Magnesium Carbonate, $MgCO_3$."

MASS OF OXYGEN = 16 x 3 = 48 (since its A_r is 16 and there are three atoms of it!).

RELATIVE FORMULA MASS (M_r) of $MgCO_3$ = (A_r for Mg) 24 + (A_r for C) 12 + (A_r for O x 3) 48 = 84.

Substituting into our formula ... $\dfrac{\text{MASS OF ELEMENT}}{M_r \text{ OF COMPOUND}} \times 100$, ... we get $\frac{48}{84} \times 100 = \underline{57.1\%}$

EXAMPLE 3 "Calculate the percentage mass of Potassium in Potassium Carbonate, K_2CO_3."

MASS OF POTASSIUM = 39 x 2 = 78 (since its A_r is 39 and there are two atoms of it!).

RELATIVE FORMULA MASS (M_r) of K_2CO_3 = (A_r for K x 2) 78 + (A_r for C) 12 + (A_r for O x 3) 48 = 138.

Substituting into our formula ... $\dfrac{\text{MASS OF ELEMENT}}{M_r \text{ OF COMPOUND}} \times 100$, ... we get $\frac{78}{138} \times 100 = \underline{56.5\%}$

Summary

All we're really doing is DIVIDING THE MASS OF THE ELEMENT ...

... by the MASS OF THE COMPOUND and multiplying by 100!

- Just make sure you account for <u>all</u> the atoms in the element or compound.

A basic law of science called the law of conservation of mass ...
... states that matter cannot be created or destroyed in
a chemical reaction.

REACTANTS — PRODUCTS

This means in a reaction that:

THE TOTAL MASS OF THE REACTANTS = THE TOTAL MASS OF THE PRODUCTS

HIGHER/SPECIAL TIER

It is possible to use this idea to work out how much of a substance is used up or produced in a chemical reaction.

EXAMPLE 1 How much Calcium Oxide can be produced from 50Kg of calcium carbonate?
(Relative Atomic Masses: Ca = 40, C = 12, O = 16)

STEP 1: Write down the equation.

$$Ca\,CO_{3(s)} \xrightarrow{\text{HEAT}} Ca\,O_{(s)} + CO_{2(g)}$$

STEP 2: Work out the M_r of each substance.

$$40 + 12 + (3 \times 16) \longrightarrow (40 + 16) + [12 + (2 \times 16)]$$

STEP 3: CHECK the total mass of reactants
= the total mass of the products
If they are not the same, check your work.

$$100 \longrightarrow 56 + 44 \checkmark$$

Since the question only mentions calcium oxide and calcium carbonate, you can now ignore the carbon dioxide!

This gives us ... **THE RATIO OF MASS OF REACTANT ...** $100 \longrightarrow 56$ **... TO MASS OF PRODUCT**

STEP 4: Apply this ratio to the question ...

... If 100Kg of $CaCO_3$ produces 56Kg of CaO ...

... then 1Kg $CaCO_3$ produces $\frac{56}{100}$ Kg of CaO ...

... and 50Kg of $CaCO_3$ produces $\frac{56}{100} \times 50$ = <u>28Kg of CaO.</u>

EXAMPLE 2 How much Aluminium Oxide is needed to produce 540 tonnes of Aluminium?
(Relative Atomic Masses: Al = 27, O = 16).

STEP 1: Write down the equation.

$$2\,Al_2\,O_{3(l)} \longrightarrow 4\,Al_{(l)} + 3O_{2(g)}$$

STEP 2: Work out the M_r of each substance.

$$2[(2 \times 27) + (3 \times 16)] \longrightarrow (4 \times 27) + [3 \times (2 \times 16)]$$

STEP 3: CHECK the total mass of reactants
= the total mass of the products

$$204 \longrightarrow 108 + 96 \checkmark$$

Since the question only mentions aluminium oxide and aluminium, you can now ignore the oxygen!

This gives us ... **THE RATIO OF MASS OF REACTANT** $204 \longrightarrow 108$ **TO MASS OF PRODUCT**

STEP 4: Apply this ratio to the question ...

... If 204 tonnes of $Al_2\,O_3$ produces 108 tonnes of Al ...

... then $\frac{204}{108}$ tonnes is needed to produce 1 tonne of Al ...

... and $\frac{204}{108} \times 540$ tonnes is needed to produce 540 tonnes of Al.

i.e. <u>1020 tonnes of $Al_2\,O_3$ is needed</u>

Empirical Formula

The Empirical Formula is the simplest formula which represents the RATIO OF ATOMS IN A COMPOUND. There's one simple rule ...

ALWAYS DIVIDE THE DATA YOU ARE GIVEN BY THE A_r OF THE ELEMENT.

EXAMPLE 1 "Find the simplest formula of an oxide of Iron, formed by reacting 2.24g of Iron with 0.96g of Oxygen." (A_r: Fe = 56, O = 16.)

STEP 1: Divide masses by A_r.   For Iron $\frac{2.24}{56}$ = 0.04   For Oxygen $\frac{0.96}{16}$ = 0.06

STEP 2: Simplify this ratio.   0.04 : 0.06   becomes   2 : 3

Write formula.   **Simplest formula = Fe_2O_3**

EXAMPLE 2 "Find the simplest formula of an oxide of Magnesium which contains 60% Magnesium and 40% Oxygen by weight ." (A_r: Mg = 24, O = 16.) Just treat the percentages as if they were grams ...

STEP 1: Divide masses by A_r.   For Magnesium $\frac{60}{24}$ = 2.5   For Oxygen $\frac{40}{16}$ = 2.5

STEP 2: Simplify this ratio.   2.5 : 2.5   becomes   1 : 1

STEP 3: Write formula.   **Simplest formula = MgO**

Calculating The Volume Of Gases In Reactions

- Firstly the mass of gas is calculated in exactly the same way as on the previous page.
- Then, the mass of the gas must be converted into a volume, using this fact ...

... THE RELATIVE FORMULA MASS (M_r) OF A GAS IN GRAMS OCCUPIES A VOLUME OF 24 LITRES ...
... AT ROOM TEMPERATURE AND ATMOSPHERIC PRESSURE (R.T.P).

In other words 2 grams of Hydrogen (H_2), 32 grams of Oxygen (O_2) and 44 grams of Carbon Dioxide (CO_2) all occupy a volume of 24 litres at ordinary pressure and temperature.

EXAMPLE Determine the volume of ammonia formed when 56g of nitrogen reacts completely with hydrogen (Relative Atomic Masses: N = 14, H = 1)

STEP 1: Write down the equation. $N_2 + 3H_2 \longrightarrow 2NH_3$

STEP 2: Work out the M_r of each substance. $(2 \times 14) + 3 \times (2 \times 1) \longrightarrow 2[14 + (3 \times 1)]$

STEP 3: Check the total mass of reactants $28 + 6 \longrightarrow 34$ ✓

     = Total mass of products.

Since the question only applies to ammonia and nitrogen, you can now ignore the hydrogen!

This gives us ... THE RATIO OF MASS OF REACTANT ... $28 \longrightarrow 34$ ... TO THE MASS OF THE PRODUCT

STEP 4: Apply the ratios to the question ...   ... If 28g of nitrogen produces 34g of ammonia ...

     ... then 1g of nitrogen would produce $\frac{34}{28}$ g of ammonia ...

     ... and 56g of nitrogen would produce $\frac{34}{28} \times 56$ = 68g of ammonia

STEP 5: Convert this mass to a volume ... M_r OF A GAS IN GRAMS OCCUPIES 24 LITRES

     17g of ammonia would occupy 24 litres ...

     ... and so 1g of ammonia would occupy $\frac{24}{17}$ litres ...

     ... and 68g of ammonia would occupy $\frac{24}{17} \times 68$g = 96 litres ...

The Mole

● A **MOLE** (mol) is a MEASUREMENT of the NUMBER OF 'PARTICLES' contained in a SUBSTANCE. ONE MOLE of __ANY__ SUBSTANCE (ELEMENT or COMPOUND) WILL ALWAYS CONTAIN THE SAME NUMBER OF PARTICLES (ATOMS or MOLECULES). [Six hundred thousand billion billion or 6×10^{23}!!!]

● The **MOLAR MASS** (g/mol) is the MASS OF __ONE__ MOLE OF THAT SUBSTANCE ...
... and is ALWAYS ...
... EQUAL to the RELATIVE ATOMIC or FORMULA MASS of THAT SUBSTANCE (ELEMENT or COMPOUND) IN GRAMS.

e.g.

Aluminium
27g/mol

27g

1mol

Sulphur
32g/mol

32g

1mol

Copper Chloride
134.5g/mol

134.5g

1mol

EXAMPLE 1

What is the molar mass of carbon?
FORMULA = C
RELATIVE ATOMIC MASS, A_r of C = 12
THEREFORE MOLAR MASS OF CARBON,
M = 12g/mol.

EXAMPLE 2

What is the molar mass of carbon dioxide?
FORMULA = CO_2
RELATIVE FORMULA MASS, M_r of CO_2 = 12+(2x16)
= 44
THEREFORE MOLAR MASS OF CO_2, M = 44g/mol.

You may be asked to calculate the amount of a substance in moles ...
You can work this out by using this relationship:

$$\text{Amount of substance (mol)} = \frac{\text{mass of substance (g)}}{\text{molar mass (g/mol)}}$$

EXAMPLE 1

Calculate the number of moles
in 36g of carbon?
Using our relationship:
Amount of carbon = $\frac{36g}{12g/mol}$ ◄── MOLAR MASS
= 3 mol

EXAMPLE 2

Calculate the number of moles of carbon dioxide
in 33g of the gas?
Again using our relationship:
Amount of CO_2 = $\frac{33g}{44g/mol}$ ◄── MOLAR MASS
= 0.75 mol

Molar Volumes

Very simply ...

... ONE MOLE of any GAS at ROOM TEMP. and ATMOSPHERIC PRESS. has a VOLUME of 24 litres or dm^3 (24000 cm^3).

EXAMPLE

What volume is occupied by 88g of carbon dioxide at room temperature and atmospheric pressure?
(Molar mass of CO_2 = 44g/mol)

$$\text{Amount of } CO_2 \text{ (mol)} = \frac{\text{mass of substances (g)}}{\text{molar mass (g/mol)}} = \frac{88g}{44g/mol} = 2mol$$

1 mole of CO_2 has a volume of 24 litres.
Therefore 2 moles of CO_2 has a volume = 2 x 24 litres = 48 litres (48000 cm^3).

Bonding

- Two non-metals can share electrons to form a **COVALENT BOND** .

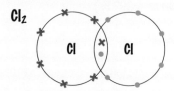
Cl_2

Cl   Cl

- Simple molecules contain strong covalent bonds between the atoms but the attraction between molecules is weak.

- Simple molecules have low melting and boiling points, do not dissolve in water and do not conduct electricity.

- Ceramics contain giant silicate molecules and are formed by heating clay.

> **HIGHER/SPECIAL TIER**
>
> - Giant molecules have strong covalent bonds throughout the whole of their structure and have very high melting and boiling points e.g. diamond and graphite.

- Metals can react with both metals and non-metals by donating an electron(s) to form an **IONIC BOND**.

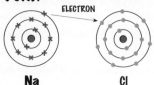
ELECTRON

Na   **Cl**

- The charged particles formed by this donating of electrons are called ions.
- Positive and negative ions attract each other to form a large ionic lattice.
- Ionic substances have high melting and boiling points, dissolve in water and conduct electricity when molten or in aqueous solution.

- When ionic substances, that are molten or dissolved in water, have electricity passed through them they break down. This is called electrolysis.

Heat

> **HIGHER/SPECIAL TIER**
>
> - At the cathode positive ions gain electrons.
> - At the anode negative ions give up electrons.

Equation Writing

- To write a formula you need to work out the correct number of positive and negative ions needed e.g. MCl_2

Mg^{2+} Cl^-Cl^- ⟶ $Mg\,Cl_2$
(two positive charges)   (two negative charges)

> **HIGHER/SPECIAL TIER**
>
> - To write a fully balanced symbol equation:
> 1. Write a word equation.
> 2. Write down the formula.
> 3. Balance the equation.
> 4. Write down the state symbols.

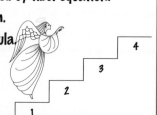

- A_r - the relative atomic mass of an element (relative to Carbon - 12)
- M_r - the relative formula mass is the sum of the A_r's of each element in a substance's formula.
- In a reaction the total mass of the reactants equals the total mass of the products.

> **HIGHER/SPECIAL TIER**
>
> - The relative formula mass of a gas occupies a volume of 24 litres (24,000 cm^3) at room temperature and atmospheric pressure.

Record the **TWELVE** 'Bonding' facts and **SIX** 'Equation Writing' facts on your tape.
Now **READ, WRITE, COVER** and **CHECK** the **EIGHTEEN** facts.

Metals And Non-Metals

Extracting Metals From Ores

METALLIC BONDING

Metals are giant structures containing positive metal ions in a sea of electrons.

PROPERTIES OF NON-METALS

NON-METALS

- Low melting and boiling points (except graphite and diamond).
- Dull and brittle.
- Do not conduct electricity (except graphite).
- Acidic oxides.

RUSTING

- For iron to rust both oxygen and water are required.
- Methods for preventing rusting include painting, oiling, alloying and galvanising.

PROPERTIES OF METALS

- Have high melting and boiling points.
- Good conductors of electricity and heat.
- Shiny and malleable.
- Form alloys.
- Form basic oxides.

REDUCTION BY CARBON/ CARBON MONOXIDE

- Haematite (iron ore), limestone and coke are fed into the top of the blast furnace.
- Carbon Monoxide removes the Oxygen from iron oxide to leave iron.

$$Fe_2O_{3(s)} + 3CO_{(g)} \longrightarrow 2Fe_{(l)} + 3CO_{2(g)}$$

REACTIVITY OF METALS

Metals can be placed in order of their reactivity based on reactions with ...

- AIR (OXYGEN)
- WATER
- DILUTE ACIDS

PURIFYING COPPER

- Once copper ore has been reduced by Carbon to produce copper ...
- ... the copper is purified by electrolysis.

DISPLACEMENT REACTIONS

- A more reactive metal displaces a less reactive metal from a compound.

ALKALI METALS AND HALOGENS

- Sodium Chloride is soluble in water.
- Electrolysis of brine produces Chlorine gas, Hydrogen gas and Sodium Hydroxide.

MARGARINE

- Silver Nitrate can be used to identify halide ions.

REDUCTION BY ELECTROLYSIS

- Aluminium is too reactive to be extracted from its ore by heating with Carbon.
- Aluminium Oxide is mixed with cryolite (to lower its melting point) then electrolysed.

$$Cathode \quad Al^{3+}_{(l)} + 3e^- \longrightarrow Al_{(l)}$$

- ADVANTAGES OF MINERAL EXTRACTION - raw materials, jobs, money for local economies.
- DISADVANTAGES OF MINERAL EXTRACTION - damage to the general environment and habitats.
- The best mining companies try to reduce the environmental impact of mining.
- When LOCATING A CHEMICAL PLANT a company must ensure it can easily obtain its raw materials, have a good communications network and skilled workforce.

Properties Of Metals

More than three quarters of the elements are metals. They are found on the left hand side of the periodic table.

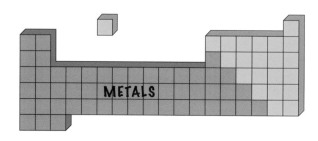

METALS

PROPERTIES OF METALS	USES OF METALS
● Have high melting and boiling points. All are solids at room temperature (except mercury which is a liquid). ● Good conductors of heat and electricity when solid or liquid. ● Are shiny (at least when freshly cut or just after polishing). ● They are malleable (can be bent and hammered into shape). ● Usually hard and strong. ● Form alloys (mixtures of metals).	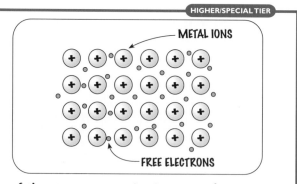 Iron can be used to make pans. Copper is used for electrical wiring. Duralumin is used to make aircraft bodies (an alloy containing low density aluminium).

An important ⌐CHEMICAL PROPERTY⌐ of metals is that they react with oxygen to form ⌐BASIC OXIDES⌐ e.g. sodium oxide, calcium oxide ...

HIGHER/SPECIAL TIER

● Metals have a giant structure ...
   ... in which electrons in the highest energy level ...
   ... become free to move through the whole structure ...
   This effectively produces ...
   ... a regular arrangement (lattice) of metal ions ...
   ... in a "sea of electrons".

METAL IONS

FREE ELECTRONS

● Metals tend to have high melting and boiling points because of the strong attraction between the positive metal ions and negative electrons.

● Metals are malleable because the layers of metal ions can slide relative to each other.

● Metals conduct electricity because the electrons are free to flow through the giant lattice.

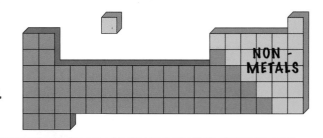

Properties

Less than a quarter of the elements in the
Periodic Table are non-metals.
They are found on the right hand side of the Periodic Table.

PROPERTIES OF NON-METALS

- Generally have low melting and boiling points (except graphite and diamond, which are forms of carbon and have very high melting and boiling points). Half the non-metallic elements are gases at room temperature and bromine is a liquid.

- They are mostly dull.

- Usually brittle (snap when being bent or hammered) and crumble easily when solid.

- Are poor conductors of heat and electricity (except graphite which conducts electricity).

An important CHEMICAL PROPERTY of non-metals is that they react with oxygen to form ACIDIC OXIDES e.g. sulphur dioxide, carbon dioxide, oxides of nitrogen ...

CARBON DIOXIDE
SULPHUR DIOXIDE ⟶ dissolve in water to form ACIDS.
NITROGEN DIOXIDE

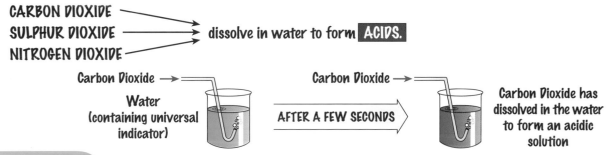

Carbon Dioxide ⟶
Water (containing universal indicator)

AFTER A FEW SECONDS

Carbon Dioxide ⟶

Carbon Dioxide has dissolved in the water to form an acidic solution

The Halides

- If a HALOGEN ATOM gains an electron ...
  ... it forms a negatively charged HALIDE ION e.g. chloride ion, bromide ion.
- When silver nitrate is added to a solution containing a halide ion (e.g. Cl^-, Br^-) then a precipitation reaction occurs.

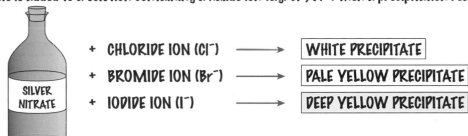

SILVER NITRATE

+ CHLORIDE ION (Cl^-) ⟶ WHITE PRECIPITATE

+ BROMIDE ION (Br^-) ⟶ PALE YELLOW PRECIPITATE

+ IODIDE ION (I^-) ⟶ DEEP YELLOW PRECIPITATE

HIGHER/SPECIAL TIER

EXAMPLE:

POTASSIUM CHLORIDE + SILVER NITRATE ⟶ SILVER CHLORIDE + POTASSIUM NITRATE

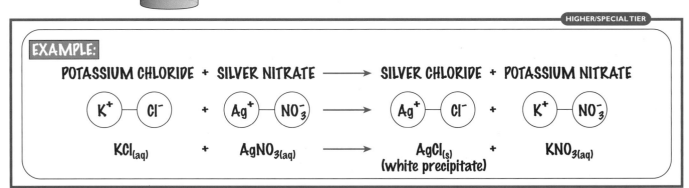

K^+ — Cl^- + Ag^+ — NO_3^- ⟶ Ag^+ — Cl^- + K^+ — NO_3^-

$KCl_{(aq)}$ + $AgNO_{3(aq)}$ ⟶ $AgCl_{(s)}$ + $KNO_{3(aq)}$
(white precipitate)

The Reactivity Series Of Metals

By observing how metals react with OXYGEN (air), WATER and DILUTE ACIDS, we can place them in order of how reactive they are. This is called the REACTIVITY SERIES.

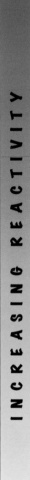

INCREASING REACTIVITY

ELEMENT	REACTION WITH OXYGEN (AIR)	REACTION WITH WATER	REACTION WITH DILUTE ACID
POTASSIUM	BURNS BRIGHTLY WHEN HEATED TO FORM OXIDE (SODIUM)	VERY VIGOROUS REACTION IN COLD WATER FORMS HYDROXIDE (HYDROGEN GAS, POTASSIUM, WATER)	VIOLENT REACTION AND VERY DANGEROUS
SODIUM			
CALCIUM	BURNS BRIGHTLY IN AIR WHEN HEATED TO FORM OXIDE (MAGNESIUM, BUNSEN BURNER)	REACTS WITH STEAM BUT NOT WATER TO FORM OXIDE (HYDROGEN, STEAM, IRON)	REASONABLE REACTION WHICH DECREASES AS WE GO DOWN THE SERIES (HYDROGEN GAS, MAGNESIUM)
MAGNESIUM			
ALUMINIUM	REACT SLOWLY WHEN HEATED TO FORM OXIDE (COPPER, BUNSEN BURNER)		
CARBON			
ZINC			
IRON			
HYDROGEN			
COPPER			
SILVER	NO REACTION (SILVER, BUNSEN BURNER)	NO REACTION WITH WATER OR STEAM (COPPER)	NO REACTION (GOLD)
GOLD			

Reaction With Air

- Most metals react with oxygen to form an oxide.
- Metal oxides are basic (the chemical opposite of an acid).

$$METAL \ + \ OXYGEN \longrightarrow METAL \ OXIDES.$$

Test for hydrogen gas

HYDROGEN

LIGHTED SPLINT

POP!!!

'Pops' when a lighted splint is put in.

Reactions With Water

- Potassium, sodium and calcium all react with cold water to produce a metal **HYDROXIDE** and hydrogen gas.
- Magnesium will react slowly with cold water but it reacts much faster with steam.
- Magnesium, aluminium, zinc and iron all react with steam to produce a metal **OXIDE** and hydrogen gas.

$$METAL \ + \ WATER \longrightarrow METAL \ HYDROXIDE \ or \ METAL \ OXIDE \ + \ HYDROGEN$$

Reactions With Dilute Acids

- Many metals react with dilute acids to produce a salt and hydrogen gas.

$$METAL \ + \ ACID \longrightarrow METAL \ SALT \ + \ HYDROGEN$$

Displacement Reactions

A **DISPLACEMENT REACTION** is one in which a more reactive metal displaces a less reactive metal from a compound in a chemical reaction.

An iron nail is put in a beaker of Copper Sulphate solution.

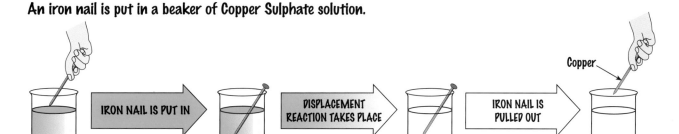

IRON NAIL IS PUT IN → DISPLACEMENT REACTION TAKES PLACE → IRON NAIL IS PULLED OUT → Copper

If we look at the POSITIONS of IRON and COPPER in the REACTIVITY SERIES ...
... we can explain what happens.

The more REACTIVE Iron ...   ... takes the sulphate from the copper ...   ... to form iron sulphate ...   ... and copper.

There is one simple rule to remember:

> **A METAL HIGHER UP THE REACTIVITY SERIES (MORE REACTIVE) WILL DISPLACE A LESS REACTIVE METAL FROM ITS COMPOUND.**

Some More Examples Of Displacement?

EXAMPLE No. 1

ZINC + COPPER SULPHATE SOLUTION
Remember the "Rule". Which is HIGHER in the Reactivity series?

ZINC + COPPER SULPHATE ⟶ ZINC SULPHATE + COPPER
Yes! Zinc is higher so it displaces the copper forming Zinc Sulphate.

EXAMPLE No. 2

COPPER + MAGNESIUM NITRATE SOLUTION
Remember the "Rule". Which is HIGHER in the Reactivity series?

COPPER + MAGNESIUM NITRATE ⟶ MAGNESIUM NITRATE + COPPER
No! Copper is lower in the series than Magnesium so no reaction takes place.

Alkali metals react with halogens to form IONIC COMPOUNDS. The best example is sodium chloride ...
... which dissolves in water to give a colourless solution.

Industrial Electrolysis Of Brine

Brine is a very concentrated solution of sodium chloride and when it is electrolysed ...

- CHLORINE GAS
- HYDROGEN GAS
- and SODIUM HYDROXIDE SOLUTION are produced.

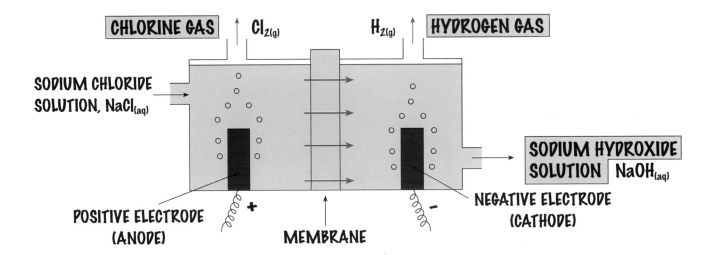

How The Products Are Used

The products of the electrolysis of sodium chloride have many uses:

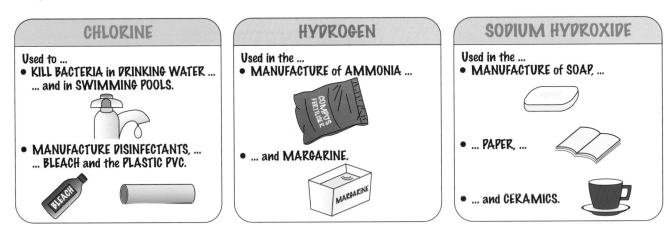

CHLORINE	HYDROGEN	SODIUM HYDROXIDE
Used to ... ● KILL BACTERIA in DRINKING WATER ... ... and in SWIMMING POOLS. ● MANUFACTURE DISINFECTANTS, ... BLEACH and the PLASTIC PVC.	Used in the ... ● MANUFACTURE of AMMONIA ... ● ... and MARGARINE.	Used in the ... ● MANUFACTURE of SOAP, ... ● ... PAPER, ... ● ... and CERAMICS.

You also need to know the laboratory test for Chlorine, which is ...
... that it BLEACHES DAMP LITMUS PAPER (i.e. removes the colour).

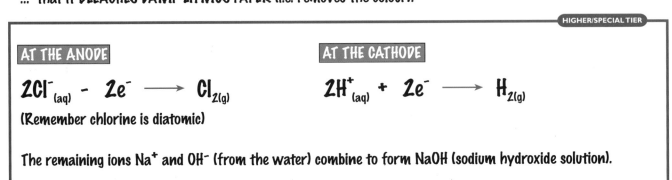

AT THE ANODE

$$2Cl^-_{(aq)} - 2e^- \longrightarrow Cl_{2(g)}$$

(Remember chlorine is diatomic)

AT THE CATHODE

$$2H^+_{(aq)} + 2e^- \longrightarrow H_{2(g)}$$

The remaining ions Na^+ and OH^- (from the water) combine to form NaOH (sodium hydroxide solution).

- The Earth's Crust contains many naturally occurring elements and compounds called MINERALS.
- A METAL ORE is a mineral or mixture of minerals from which economically viable amounts of pure metal can be extracted.
- Most ores are either METAL OXIDES or METAL SULPHIDES.
- To extract the metal from a metal oxide then the OXYGEN MUST BE REMOVED.
- The removal of OXYGEN is called REDUCTION.
- The METHOD OF EXTRACTION depends on the metals' position in the REACTIVITY SERIES.

REACTIVITY SERIES	METHOD OF EXTRACTION	MAIN INDUSTRIAL PROCESS
Potassium Sodium Calcium Magnesium Aluminium	The metals are all reactive and a great deal of energy is required to extract them from their ores. ELECTROLYSIS is used. Metal ions gain electrons at the cathode.	Electrolysis of Aluminium Oxide
Zinc Iron Copper	These metals are below carbon in the reactivity series and are extracted from their ores by heating with carbon/carbon monoxide.	Reduction of Iron Oxide in the BLAST FURNACE
Silver Gold	These metals are unreactive and exist NATURALLY. They are obtained by physical processes eg panning.	

Mining For Metal Ores

STEP 1: GEOLOGISTS look at data from geomagnetic and mineral exploration studies to find the most likely sites of certain minerals (eg metal ores).

STEP 2: MINING begins and ORES are extracted. The ORES will be crushed and waste material is removed so that the metal compound becomes more concentrated.

STEP 3: The metal is extracted from the ORE.

HIGHER/SPECIAL TIER

ADVANTAGES OF MINERAL EXTRACTION	DISADVANTAGES OF MINERAL EXTRACTION
• Valuable raw materials can be extracted to make useful products. • The mining industry provides jobs for people. • The wages spent by people working in mineral extraction can help the local economy.	• Excessive mining can continually remove minerals from the Earth's Crust which are not replaced. • Mining can damage the environment by producing large quarries, spoilheaps and noise. • Mining can ruin or damage habitats.

The best mining companies try to reduce the environmental impact of mineral extraction by ...

1. Planting tree breaks to reduce visual impact of the quarry and the noise from traffic.

2. Landscaping the site once mining has finished to provide new facilities and habitats.

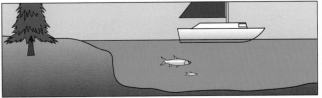

Extracting Iron - The Blast Furnace

Iron is one of the most widely used metals in the world
... for building, transport and everyday objects.

Haematite is the name of the ore from which iron is extracted.
It contains IRON OXIDE.

IRON ORE, LIMESTONE AND COKE

WASTE GASES

HOT AIR

HIGH TEMPERATURE and CARBON are used here to extract IRON from its ORE.

molten slag tapped here

HOT AIR via the tuyeres

molten iron tapped here

- HAEMATITE (iron ore), limestone and coke (carbon)
  are fed into the top of the furnace ...
  ... hot air is blasted in at the bottom.

- The CARBON REACTS WITH OXYGEN to form
  CARBON DIOXIDE and a great deal of heat.

- The carbon dioxide will react with more carbon
  to form carbon monoxide.

- CARBON MONOXIDE IS A REDUCING AGENT and will
  take the oxygen from the iron oxide leaving just iron.

> IRON OXIDE + CARBON MONOXIDE ⟶ IRON + CARBON DIOXIDE

The limestone reacts with impurities, including sand, to form the slag.

Basic Oxygen Process

- The iron produced in the Blast Furnace contains quite a bit of carbon which ...
  ... makes the iron very brittle.

- Oxygen can be blown through the molten iron ...
  ... and reacts with the carbon producing carbon dioxide ...
  ... leaving a much more malleable, low carbon form of iron called steel.

HIGHER/SPECIAL TIER

These are the symbol equations for the reactions in the blast furnace. See if you can match them to the correct stages above:

(1) $C_{(s)} + O_{2(g)} \longrightarrow CO_{2(g)} +$ HEAT

(2) $CO_{2(g)} + C_{(s)} \longrightarrow 2CO_{(g)}$

(3) $Fe_2O_{3(s)} + 3CO_{(g)} \longrightarrow 2Fe_{(l)} + 3CO_{2(g)}$

(4) $CaCO_{3(s)} \xrightarrow{\text{HEAT}} CaO_{(s)} + CO_{2(g)}$
Limestone

(5) $CaO_{(s)} + SiO_{2(s)} \longrightarrow CaSiO_{3(l)}$
(Basic Oxide) (Acidic Oxide)   Slag

(The reaction between calcium oxide and silicon dioxide is a neutralisation reaction)

The Rusting Of Iron

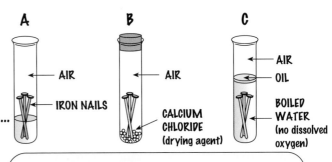

When iron reacts with water and oxygen ...
- ... rust (hydrated iron (III) oxide) is formed ...
- ... and this weakens the iron.
- Rusting is an example of an OXIDATION REACTION ...
  ... but it is not very useful to us!

BOTH OXYGEN AND WATER are needed for rusting.
Salt (sodium chloride) can speed up the rate of rusting.

THREE DAYS LATER ...
A - RUST   B - NO RUST   C - NO RUST

METHOD OF PREVENTING RUSTING	FURTHER EXPLANATIONS
● PAINTING 	● This can be used to cover very large surfaces like bridges and ships. Paint acts as a barrier between the iron and water/oxygen.
● OILING	● Oiling is very useful on moving parts as it prevents rusting and lubricates the machinery. Oil repels water.
● ALLOYING	● When iron is mixed with chromium and nickel then stainless steel is formed. Stainless steel does not rust.
● GALVANISING (covering iron with a thin layer of zinc)	● Zinc is a more reactive metal than iron and will react with water/oxygen in preference to the iron (SACRIFICIAL PROTECTION). The zinc will protect the iron even when the zinc surface has been scratched.

Purifying Copper

Copper is extracted from its ore by REDUCTION ...
... but the copper obtained contains impurities.
However, pure copper can be obtained by ELECTROLYSIS.
AT THE POSITIVE ANODE copper atoms change into copper
ions and dissolve in the solution. Impurities fall to the bottom
of the tank.
AT THE NEGATIVE CATHODE positive copper ions are attracted
and change into copper atoms (the pure metal).
Very similar apparatus can be used to copper plate an object ...
... with the object being made into the negative cathode where a thin layer of copper metal becomes deposited on it.

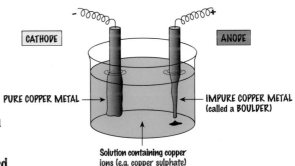

CATHODE   ANODE

PURE COPPER METAL   IMPURE COPPER METAL (called a BOULDER)

Solution containing copper ions (e.g. copper sulphate)

HIGHER/SPECIAL TIER

AT THE ANODE

$$Cu_{(s)} - 2e^- \longrightarrow Cu^{2+}_{(aq)}$$

Impure Copper   Copper Ions in solution

AT THE CATHODE

$$Cu^{2+}_{(aq)} + 2e^- \longrightarrow Cu_{(s)}$$

Pure Copper

OXIDATION Is Loss O I L
OF ELECTRONS.

REDUCTION Is Gain R I G
OF ELECTRONS.

Reactions involving both OXIDATION and REDUCTION are called REDOX reactions.

Extracting Aluminium By Electrolysis

- Aluminium is obtained from its ore by electrolysis because ...
  ... it is too reactive to be extracted by heating with carbon.
  (Look at the reactivity series on page 41: Aluminium is higher up the series than carbon).
- ALUMINIUM ORE (BAUXITE) is purified to leave aluminium oxide.
- Aluminium oxide is MIXED WITH CRYOLITE TO LOWER ITS MELTING POINT.
- The Aluminium oxide and cryolite mixture is melted ...
  ... so that the IONS CAN MOVE.

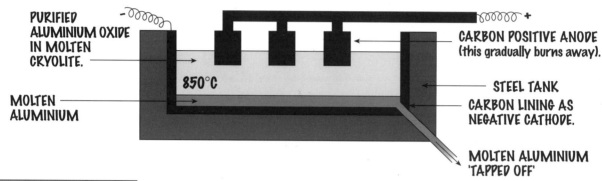

PURIFIED ALUMINIUM OXIDE IN MOLTEN CRYOLITE.

CARBON POSITIVE ANODE (this gradually burns away).

850°C

STEEL TANK
CARBON LINING AS NEGATIVE CATHODE.

MOLTEN ALUMINIUM

MOLTEN ALUMINIUM 'TAPPED OFF'

AT THE POSITIVE ANODE:

Negative oxide ions are attracted and changed into oxygen gas.
Some of the oxygen gas reacts with the graphite (carbon) electrode to give carbon dioxide ...
... so the graphite anodes need to be regularly replaced.

AT THE NEGATIVE CATHODE:

Positive aluminium ions are attracted and gain electrons to form aluminium atoms.
Lots of ENERGY is needed to produce aluminium - HEAT to convert solid aluminium oxide (and cryolite) into a liquid and ELECTRICITY for electrolysis.

AT THE ANODE

$$2O^{2-}_{(l)} - 4e^- \longrightarrow O_{2(g)}$$

(Remember gaseous oxygen is diatomic)

AT THE CATHODE

$$Al^{3+}_{(l)} + 3e^- \longrightarrow Al_{(l)}$$

Locating An Aluminium Smelter Or Blast Furnace

When industrialist are deciding the best place to put their chemical plant they need to think of a number of factors.

LOCATING AN ALUMINIUM SMELTER	LOCATING A BLAST FURNACE
• Near to a plentiful supply of cheap electricity (e.g. near a Hydro-electric power station).	• Near a plentiful supply of coal to make coke - (e.g. near a coal field)
• Near a port - both Haematite and Bauxite are imported into Britain.	
• Good communication network - road and rail links are vital to import raw materials and export products.	
• Skilled work force.	

Metals And Non-metals

METALS

- Metals have high melting and boiling points, are good conductors of heat and electricity, are shiny, malleable and form alloys.
- Metals have basic oxides.

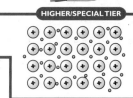

- Metals consist of a giant lattice of metal ions surrounded by a "sea of electrons" that are free to move.
- Metals can be placed in a Reactivity series based on their reactions with air, water and dilute acids.
- A more reactive metal will displace a less reactive metal from a compound in a DISPLACEMENT REACTION.

NON-METALS

- Non-metals have low melting and boiling points, are dull, and brittle.
- They do not conduct electricity (except graphite) or heat.
- Non-metals have acidic oxides.

ALKALI METALS AND HALOGENS

- Brine (Sodium Chloride solution) can be electrolysed to produce Chlorine gas, Hydrogen gas and Sodium Hydroxide solution.
- Hydrogen is used to make ammonia and margarine.
- Chlorine is used to kill bacteria, make disinfectants, bleaches and PVC.
- Sodium hydroxide is used to make soap, paper and ceramics.
- Silver nitrate can be used to test for halide ions.

Extracting Metals From Ores

- Metals are extracted from their ores by reduction.
- For metals above carbon in the reactivity series electrolysis is used. (eg. aluminium).
- For metals below carbon in the reactivity series the ore is reduced by carbon or carbon monoxide (eg. Iron).
- Iron will rust if both oxygen and water are present.
- Methods of preventing rusting include painting, oiling, alloying and galvanising.
- When copper has been extracted from its ore it can be purified by electrolysis.

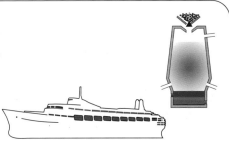

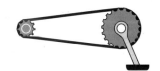

- There are both advantages and disadvantages to extracting minerals from the Earth's Crust (you must know both).
- When locating a chemical plant a company needs to consider how it gets its raw materials, the need for a good communications network and a skilled workforce.

Record the THIRTEEN 'Metals and Non-metals' facts and EIGHT 'Extracting Metals from Ores' facts onto your tape.
Now - READ, COVER, WRITE and CHECK the TWENTY ONE facts.

Crude Oil And Its Products

USES OF THE FRACTIONS

● The fractions of crude oil are used as fuel for cooking, cars, aircraft and heating.

● They also have many other important uses: e.g. plastics, cosmetics and medicines.

SEPARATING CRUDE OIL

● Crude oil is a mixture of hydrocarbons.

● It is separated by fractional distillation.

● The separate fractions have different boiling points.

SEARCH FOR CRUDE OIL

● New oil supplies have to be found as it runs out.

● Oil is found in layers of sedimentary rock.

HIGHER/SPECIAL TIER

● Seismic Surveys give a picture of the rock structure.

● Drilling is used to check for the presence of oil.

FORMATION OF CRUDE OIL

● Coal, oil and gas are fossil fuels.

● Oil is formed over millions of years by the action of heat and pressure on dead sea creatures.

● Oil is a finite, non-renewable fuel, one day it will run out.

HYDROCARBONS

● Small chain hydrocarbon molecules have low boiling points and are pale, flammable, non viscous liquids or gases.

● Long chain hydrocarbon molecules have high boiling points, and are dark, viscous liquids or waxy solids.

● Hydrocarbons contain only Hydrogen + Carbon.

● Methane is the smallest hydrocarbon.

● The size of a hydrocarbon molecule affects its properties.

ALKANES

● Hydrocarbons containing only single bonds.

HIGHER/SPECIAL TIER

● Saturated compounds.

● Formula C_nH_{2n+2}

● First 4 Alkanes, Methane, Ethane, Propane, Butane.

● These are all fuels.

● Methane is the main constituent of natural gas.

HIGHER/SPECIAL TIER

● Alkanes with 4 or more carbons can form isomers.

CRACKING

● Long chain alkanes are not very useful.

● Cracking breaks them into smaller more useful molecules.

ALKENES

● Hydrocarbons containing one double bond.

● First 2 alkenes, Ethene, propene.

● Undergo addition reactions.

● Test for alkenes, brown bromine water goes colourless.

MORE ORGANIC COMPOUNDS

HIGHER/SPECIAL TIER

—O—H

—C=O

—O—C—

—C=O
        H

—C=O
        O—H

● Alcohols – solvents.

● Esters – flavourings.

● Sugars – sweeteners (aldehydes) preservatives

● acids – preservatives.

POLYMERS

● Small alkene monomers undergo addition reactions. (Addition Polymerisation)

● Long chain addition polymers like polyethene) are produced.

HIGHER/SPECIAL TIER

$$n \begin{pmatrix} H & H \\ | & | \\ C=C \\ | & | \\ H & H \end{pmatrix} \rightarrow \begin{pmatrix} H & H \\ | & | \\ C-C \\ | & | \\ H & H \end{pmatrix}_n$$

● Different polymers have different properties and uses.

● Thermosoftening plastics can be remoulded

● Thermosetting plastics cannot be remoulded.

Formation Of Crude Oil

- Crude Oil, Coal and Natural gas are FOSSIL FUELS.
- These are fuels that have formed over MILLIONS of years ...
- ... by the action of HEAT and PRESSURE ...
- ... on ORGANIC materials from ANIMALS and PLANTS.

Crude Oil and Natural Gas were formed from animals that live in the sea.

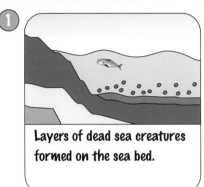

Layers of dead sea creatures formed on the sea bed.

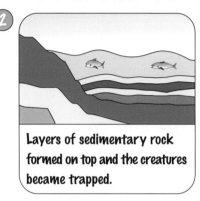

Layers of sedimentary rock formed on top and the creatures became trapped.

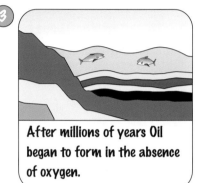

After millions of years Oil began to form in the absence of oxygen.

- Natural Gas is usually formed with Crude Oil.

Our supplies of fossil fuels were formed millions of years ago - once we have used them up we can never get them back. Resources like this are known as:

FINITE because there is not an endless supply.

Or NON-RENEWABLE because once they are gone they're gone forever.

The Search For Oil

Crude Oil is a very valuable resource - it has many different uses.

Our Crude Oil supplies are running out and are difficult to find.

Oil companies have to search for clues that might lead them to a new oil supply.

CLUE 1 ROCK FORMATION

Oil is often formed under a FOLD in the sedimentary rock like this.

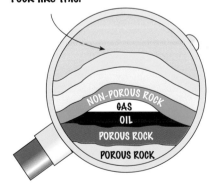

- Oil and Gas are less dense than water ...
- ... and so rise up through layers of porous rocks ...
- until they reach a layer of non-porous rock.

HIGHER/SPECIAL TIER

CLUE 2 SEISMIC SURVEYS

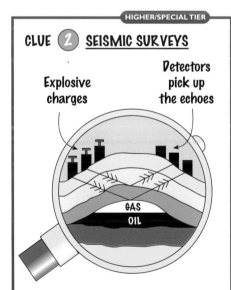

Explosive charges

Detectors pick up the echoes

- The shock waves from the explosions bounce off the rocks and ...
- ... the echoes are analysed by a computer to produce a 'picture' of the rock structure.

CLUE 3 DRILLING

Small wells are drilled

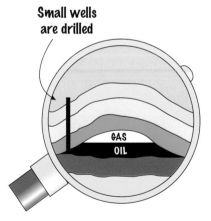

- Scientists have to drill down to prove that the rocks contain Oil ...
- ... if they do, then more wells can be drilled.

The Fractionating Column

- When Crude Oil has been extracted it is a thick, black, sticky liquid.
- It is transported to the refinery by Pipeline or by Oil Tankers.
- This is a dangerous procedure - if an accident happens and the oil spills into the sea, the effect on the wild life can be devastating.

- The Crude Oil is a MIXTURE of substances called HYDROCARBONS.
- Different hydrocarbons have different BOILING POINTS ...
- ... and so they can be separated by FRACTIONAL DISTILLATION into their individual parts or FRACTIONS.

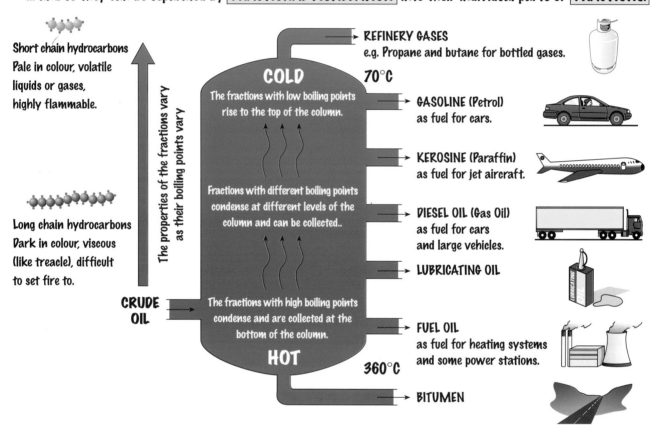

Short chain hydrocarbons Pale in colour, volatile liquids or gases, highly flammable.

Long chain hydrocarbons Dark in colour, viscous (like treacle), difficult to set fire to.

The properties of the fractions vary as their boiling points vary

COLD 70°C
The fractions with low boiling points rise to the top of the column.

Fractions with different boiling points condense at different levels of the column and can be collected..

CRUDE OIL

The fractions with high boiling points condense and are collected at the bottom of the column.

HOT 360°C

REFINERY GASES
e.g. Propane and butane for bottled gases.

GASOLINE (Petrol)
as fuel for cars.

KEROSINE (Paraffin)
as fuel for jet aircraft.

DIESEL OIL (Gas Oil)
as fuel for cars and large vehicles.

LUBRICATING OIL

FUEL OIL
as fuel for heating systems and some power stations.

BITUMEN

Uses Of The Fractions

The fractions of Crude Oil have many uses. Not just as fuels but also as a source of chemicals used to produce a wide range of products that we use every day.
If we use too much oil for fuel - there will be none left to make these essential items.

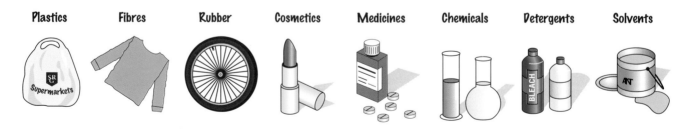

Plastics   Fibres   Rubber   Cosmetics   Medicines   Chemicals   Detergents   Solvents

The other fossil fuels - Coal and Natural Gas are also sources of useful products, besides being good fuels.

Natural Gas (methane) - as a source of hydrogen in the production of ammonia.

Coal - as a source of coke used in the production of iron.

The Fractions Of Crude Oil - A Closer Look

- The fractions of Crude Oil have many different uses because each fraction has different PROPERTIES. We can explain these properties by looking at the structure of the MOLECULES.

- The compounds in Crude Oil are mainly HYDROCARBONS.

- A hydrocarbon is a compound containing ONLY CARBON and HYDROGEN atoms, tightly bonded together in molecules.

Methane CH_4 is the shortest HYDROCARBON.

- Some hydrocarbons are very small like methane. Others can contain many carbon atoms bonded together in long chains.

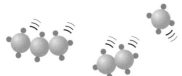

Small hydrocarbons

large hydrocarbons

Low boiling points, pale in colour, volatile liquids or gases, highly flammable.

High boiling points, dark in colour, thick viscous liquids or waxy solids, less flammable.

- The size of a hydrocarbon molecule affects the properties of the compound this is because:

HIGHER/SPECIAL TIER

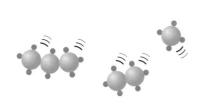

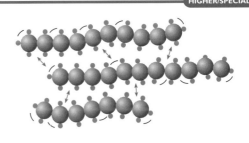

Small molecules have very SMALL FORCES between them. These forces are easy to break by heating and hydrocarbons with small molecules are volatile liquids or gases with low boiling points.

Large molecules have many more of these small forces between them, resulting in an overall LARGE FORCE. This force is more difficult to break by heating and hydrocarbons with large molecules are thick viscous liquids or waxy solids with higher boiling points.

Not all hydrocarbons have STRAIGHT chain molecules - some have BRANCHES and this can affect their properties too.

Alkanes - Single Bonds Only

- There are a number of different families of hydrocarbons.
- They are all made up of hydrogen and carbon atoms ...
- ... bonded together with strong COVALENT BONDS.
- The simplest family of hydrocarbons is the ALKANE FAMILY.
- The alkanes consist of carbon and carbon or carbon and hydrogen atoms bonded together with SINGLE BONDS.

Hydrogen atoms can make
1 BOND EACH

Carbon atoms can make
4 BONDS EACH

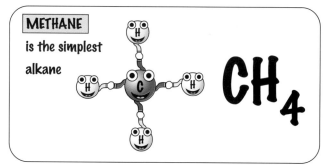

METHANE is the simplest alkane

CH_4

The next three members of the alkane family are ETHANE C_2H_6, PROPANE C_3H_8 and BUTANE C_4H_{10}.
They are all used as FUELS with methane being the main constituent of natural gas we use at home.
It is a odourless gas but has a smell added so that leaks can be detected.
In the event of a leak then DO NOT use electrical switches or light a match and call the gas company immediately.

Structural Formulae Of The Alkanes

You can write down the structural formula of any alkane by making sure that the carbon always makes four single bonds and the hydrogen only makes one.

Alkane	Structural Formula	Molecular Formula
Methane	H—C—H (with H above and below)	CH_4
Ethane	H—C—C—H (with H's)	C_2H_6
Propane	H—C—C—C—H (with H's)	C_3H_8
Butane	H—C—C—C—C—H (with H's)	C_4H_{10}

ISOMERS Alkanes which contain 4 or more carbon atoms can have more than one structure or ISOMER.
e.g. Butane

C_4H_{10} — different structural formula → C_4H_{10}
← same molecular formula →

The general formula for alkanes is $C_n H_{2n+2}$

- The Alkanes are known as SATURATED hydrocarbons because ...
- ... the carbon atoms are bonded together with SINGLE covalent bonds ...
- ... meaning there are no spare bonds left.

METHANE is the simplest alkane and is an important fuel. It is the main constituent of NATURAL GAS, MARSH GAS and gas from LAND FILL SITES where organic matter is decaying.
It is important that we look at other sources of methane, such as gas from decaying rubbish, because our supplies of natural gases will soon run out.

Alkenes - Always Have A Double Bond

- The ALKENES are another family of hydrocarbons. They are very similar to the alkanes ...
- ... except that two of the carbon atoms are joined by a DOUBLE COVALENT BOND.
- The simplest alkene is ETHENE. C_2H_4
- Alkenes will DECOLOURISE bromine water, from brown to colourless.

HIGHER/SPECIAL TIER

- All alkenes have the general formula C_nH_{2n}

Alkenes contain a double bond

or

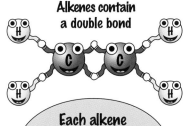

C_2H_4

The next alkene in the family is PROPENE.

Structural Formula	Molecular Formula
H—C=C—H (with CH group below)	C_3H_6

Each alkene contains one double carbon = carbon bond.

The alkenes are known as UNSATURATED hydrocarbons because of the presence of a DOUBLE covalent bond between two carbon atoms.

Some vegetable oils contain lots of double bonds - they are POLYUNSATURATED.

Addition Reactions

- The double bond in alkenes makes them more REACTIVE than alkanes.
- In a chemical reaction the double bond can be broken and new atoms or molecules added.
- These are called addition reactions.

  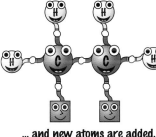

The double bond is broken ...   ... and new atoms are added.

As mentioned above, one of these addition reactions can be used to test for an unsaturated compound.

e.g. an alkene

Ethene (colourless gas)   + $Br_{2 (aq)}$ →   Dibromoethane (colourless)

Bromine Water (brown solution)

Alkenes also undergo addition reactions with hydrogen to make alkanes.

Ethene   + $H_{2 (g)}$ →   Ethane

Hydrogen

This type of reaction is used in the production of margarine.

Oils (unsaturated molecules) react with hydrogen to produce fats (saturated molecules).

Cracking

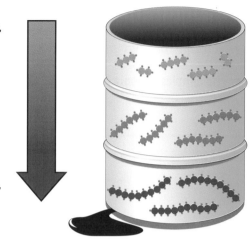

- Many of the hydrocarbons found in Crude Oil have long carbon chains.
- The greater the number of carbons in the chain:

  - The HIGHER ITS BOILING POINT is;
  - The LESS VOLATILE it is; (the less easily it vaporises)
  - The LESS EASILY IT FLOWS (the more viscous it is);
  - The LESS EASILY IT IGNITES (the less FLAMMABLE it is).

This means that these long hydrocarbons are not very useful as fuels.

Large hydrocarbon molecules can be broken down - CRACKED
- to produce SMALLER, MORE USEFUL MOLECULES.

Long chain Alkane

Broken pot catalyst   HEAT

Liquid Alkane   Cold water   Gaseous Alkene

This is the apparatus used for cracking in the laboratory.

Industrial cracking requires HIGH TEMPERATURES, HIGH PRESSURES and a CATALYST.

The short chain molecules produced during cracking are ALKENES .

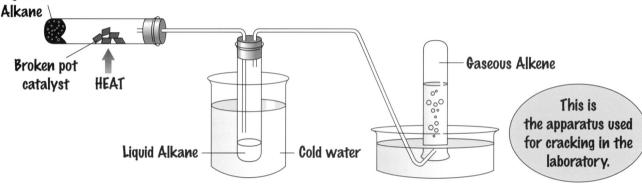

Heat / Catalyst → Ethene

Remember - we can test the alkene product using bromine water
- colour change BROWN ⟶ colourless.

Final Uses Of The Products Of Cracking

Large, less useful molecules

- The small unsaturated alkene molecules produced from cracking have many uses including their use as starting materials for the plastic and petrochemical industries.

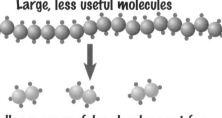

Smaller, more useful molecules used for:

- The oil refineries match their output to the demand for different products.

- The shorter chained alkanes which are produced are always in demand as fuels.

Petrol   Poly(ethene)   Polyvinyl chloride

(See P57 Addition Polymerisation)

Monomers To Polymers

- One of the important uses of the alkenes produced during cracking is the production of POLYMERS.
- Polymers are the long chain molecules that make up PLASTICS ...
- ... and ARTIFICIAL FIBRES such as nylon and polyester.

e.g. the formation of poly(ethene) from ethene.

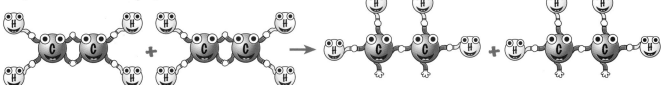

The small Alkene molecules
are called MONOMERS

The double bonds are broken

The resulting long chain molecule is
a POLYMER - in this case POLY(ETHENE)

Large numbers of
molecules can be
joined in this way.

Formulae Of Polymers

The small alkene molecules above can be described as MONOMERS. When lots of MONOMERS join together
they form a POLYMER. Because ALKENES are UNSATURATED, they are very good at joining together
and when they do so without producing another substance, we call this ADDITION POLYMERISATION.

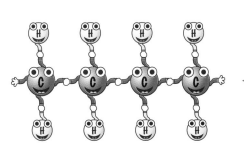

Monomer	Polymer
Ethene	Poly(ethene)
Propene	Poly(propene)

- n is the number of monomer molecules used ...
- ... and the number of repeating monomer sections in the chain.

The two examples above show alkene monomers undergoing ADDITION POLYMERISATION
in which their double bond is broken to allow the addition of other monomers
However ...

- ... Most polymers are made from alkene monomers ...
- ... in which one of the hydrogen atoms has been substituted for another atom.

e.g. Chloroethene   This produces

Poly(chloroethene)
or Polyvinylchloride (P.V.C.)
(See uses of these P58)

In industry addition polymerisation processes require HIGH PRESSURE and a CATALYST.

Uses Of Addition Polymers

- Addition polymers have a range of different PROPERTIES depending on the groups of atoms that they contain.

Polymer	Properties	Uses
Poly(ethene)	light, flexible, easily moulded	dustbins, buckets, plastic bags
Poly(propene)	strong, can be stretched into fibres	milk crates, fishing nets
Polyvinylchloride P.V.C.	tough + durable, hard (less flexible than Polyethene)	pipes, guttering, window frames
Polystyrene	light, poor conductor of heat	insulation + packaging (when expanded as foam)

Plastics are made from a valuable resource - CRUDE OIL - we should try not to waste this by disposing of plastics - RECYCLING plastic can help to solve the problems of dwindling oil supplies and the filling up of land fill sites.

- Some plastics are BIODEGRADABLE - they will decompose and rot away.
- Most plastics however are NON-BIODEGRADABLE.
- This causes problems when we throw plastics away - they can build up in land fill sites.

Thermosoftening And Thermosetting Plastics

- An important aspect of the structure of polymers is the way in which the polymer chains are held together.
- This is very important in explaining the properties of two types of plastic.

THERMOSOFTENING PLASTICS

- In these plastics the chains are held in place by quite weak INTERMOLECULAR FORCES.

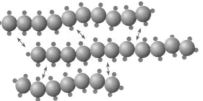

These forces are not chemical bonds and when the plastic is heated the chains can slide over one another and the plastic can be reshaped over and over again. e.g. poly(ethene).

THERMOSETTING PLASTICS

- In these plastics the chains are held in place by strong chemical bonds or CROSS LINKS between the chains.

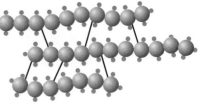

These bonds are formed during manufacturing and cannot be broken by heating.
When this type of plastic is heated it will just char and burn.

More Organic Compounds

Compounds containing long chains of carbon atoms, like those found in crude oil are called ORGANIC compounds - because they originated from organic material - PLANTS and ANIMALS.

Organic Family	Uses	Chemical Test	Functional Group
Alcohols	industrial solvents	produce sweet smelling esters on reaction with acids	$-O-H$
Aldehydes (reducing sugars)	sweeteners, preservatives, energy source	produce RED/BROWN precipitate on warming with FEHLINGS	$-C=O$ H
Acids	food preservatives	pH less than 7	$-C=O$ $O-H$
Esters	flavourings	sweet smelling	$-C=O$ $O-C-$

Families of organic chemicals can be identified by the particular groups of atoms that they contain - these are known as FUNCTIONAL GROUPS.

It is these functional groups that give different families of compounds their different CHEMICAL PROPERTIES.

Crude Oil

• **CRUDE OIL** was formed from dead sea creatures over millions of years by heat and pressure.

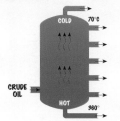

• Crude Oil is found in layers of sedimentary rock.

• Crude Oil is a mixture of **HYDROCARBONS** which can by separated by **FRACTIONAL DISTILLATION** into their individual parts or fractions.

• These fractions have many uses.

• Crude Oil is a **FINITE, NON-RENEWABLE** resource and our supplies need to be protected by using **ALTERNATIVE ENERGY** supplies and **RECYCLING** plastics.

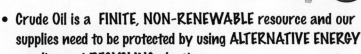

• The length of the carbon chain determines the **BOILING POINT** of a hydrocarbon.

• Hydrocarbons are useful as **FUELS** and as the starting point for many important products.

Products Of Crude Oil

• **ALKANES** are a family of hydrocarbons containing **SINGLE** bonds only.

• **ALKENES** are a family of hydrocarbons containing a **DOUBLE** bond.

HIGHER/SPECIAL TIER

• Unsaturated hydrocarbons are **REACTIVE** and undergo **ADDITION** reactions to form saturated compounds.

• Smaller more useful alkenes can be formed from long chain alkanes by **CRACKING**.

HEAT

• Alkenes can be used to produce **ADDITION POLYMERS** e.g. poly(ethene).

• The structure of polymers determines their properties. **THERMOSOFTENING** no cross links - can be remelted. **THERMOSETTING** cross linked - can't be remelted.

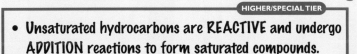

• Many other organic compounds can be produced from the hydrocarbons in crude oil.

Record the **SEVEN** 'Crude Oil' facts and **SEVEN** 'Products of Crude Oil' facts on your tape.

Now **READ, WRITE, COVER** and **CHECK** the **FOURTEEN** facts.

ENZYMES

HIGHER/SPECIAL TIER

- An enzyme is a biological catalyst.
- Specific enzymes needed for specific reactions.
- Lock and key mechanism

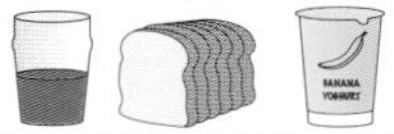

also: clarifying fruit juice, soft centred chocolates.

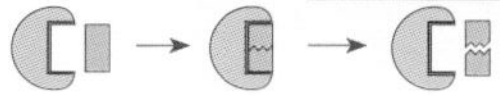

- Enzymes denatured by heat and extreme pH.
- Enzymes work best at 37°C.
- Uses:

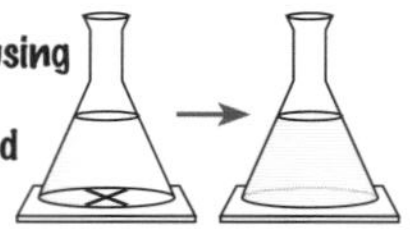

CATALYST

- Lowers the energy needed for a successful collision.
- Speeds up a reaction without being used up.
- Can be investigated using decomposition of hydrogen peroxide with Manganese (IV) Oxide catalyst.

AMMONIA

OPTIMUM CONDITIONS

350°C
450°C
550°C

60%
40%
20%

YIELD

PRESSURE/ATMOSPHERES

0   100   200   300

TEMPERATURE

SLOW

FAST

- Higher temperature results in increased rate of reaction.
- Can be investigated using reaction between hydrochloric acid and sodium thiosulphate.

Rates And Equilibrium

COLLISION THEORY

- For a chemical reaction to take place, particles must collide with sufficient energy (activation energy).
- Rate of reaction depends on the frequency of the collisions, more frequent = faster, more energetic = faster.

HABER PROCESS NITROGEN + HYDROGEN

- Optimum conditions ensure the rate is fast enough, and the yield is high enough so the cost is low.
- Ammonia is used to produce nitric acid and fertilisers.
- Too many fertilisers cause eutrophication.

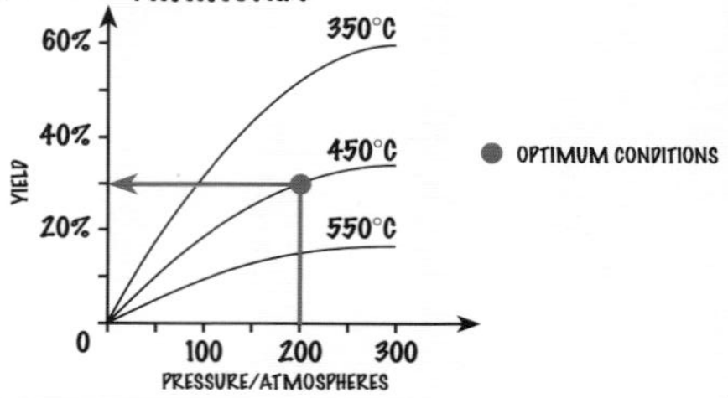

MEASURING AND ANALYSING RATES

- Measure the rate at which reactants are used up.
- Measure the rate at which products are formed.

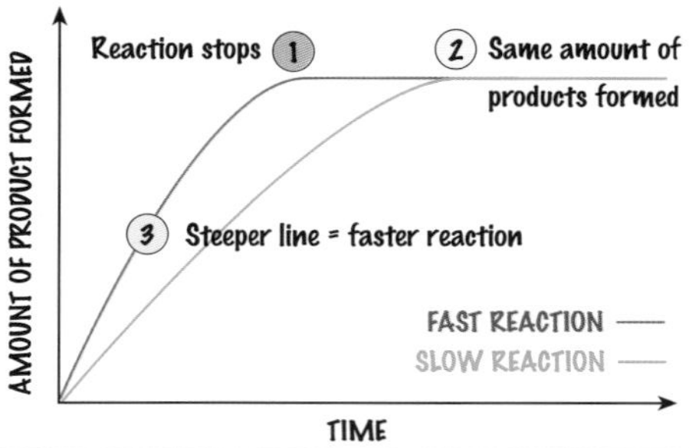

Reaction stops ①

② Same amount of products formed

③ Steeper line = faster reaction

FAST REACTION ——
SLOW REACTION ——

AMOUNT OF PRODUCT FORMED

TIME

CONCENTRATION

SLOW

FAST

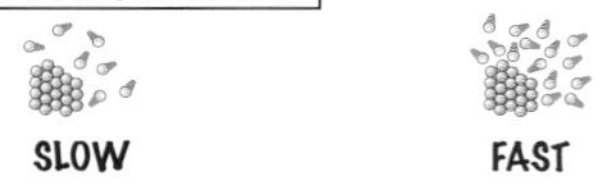

- Greater concentration results in increased rate of reaction.
- Can be investigated using reaction between hydrochloric acid and sodium thiosulphate.

DILUTE

CONCENTRATED

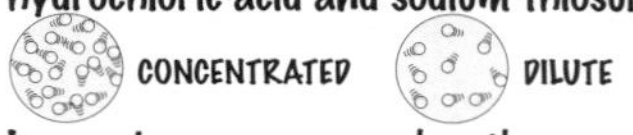

- Increasing gas pressure has the same effect.

SURFACE AREA

SLOW

FAST

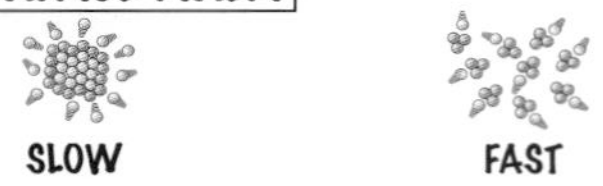

- Greater area results in increased rate of reaction.
- Can be investigated using the reactions between hydrochloric acid and large and small limestone chips.
- Large particles = small surface area.
- Small particles = large surface area.

EQUILIBRIA IN REVERSIBLE REACTIONS

- Some reactions are reversible $A + B \rightleftharpoons C + D$ + WATER

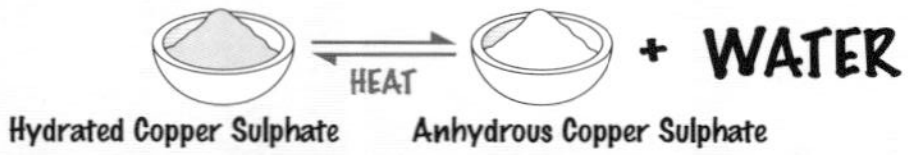

HEAT

Hydrated Copper Sulphate   Anhydrous Copper Sulphate

HIGHER/SPECIAL TIER

- If a reversible reaction takes place in a closed system an EQUILIBRIUM is set up.
- In a reversible reaction if the forward reaction is exothermic the backward reaction is endothermic.

- Chemical reactions only occur when REACTING PARTICLES COLLIDE WITH EACH OTHER ...
- ... with sufficient energy to react.
- The minimum amount of energy required to cause this reaction is called the ACTIVATION ENERGY.
- There are FOUR important factors which affect RATE OF REACTION, ...

1. Temperature Of The Reactants

When temperature increases, the PARTICLES MOVE FASTER ...

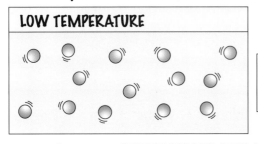

LOW TEMPERATURE

FASTER SPEED ...
... MORE COLLISIONS.

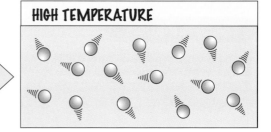

HIGH TEMPERATURE

- ... resulting in an INCREASED NUMBER OF COLLISIONS, and an INCREASED RATE OF REACTION.
- Also, the particles collide more energetically and therefore are more likely to react.

2. Concentration Of The Reactants

Increased concentration means an INCREASED NUMBER OF PARTICLES ...

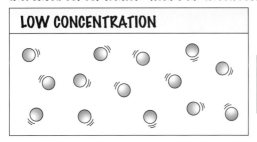

LOW CONCENTRATION

MORE PARTICLES ...
... MORE COLLISIONS.

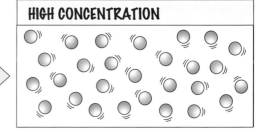

HIGH CONCENTRATION

- ... resulting in an INCREASED NUMBER OF COLLISIONS, and an INCREASED RATE OF REACTION.
- Increasing the PRESSURE of reacting GASES also increases the concentration of particles and the rate of reaction.

3. Surface Area Of Solid Reactants

Smaller pieces means a GREATER AREA FOR CONTACT ...

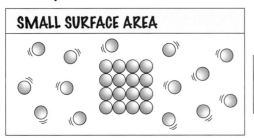

SMALL SURFACE AREA

BIGGER SURFACE AREA ...
... MORE COLLISIONS.

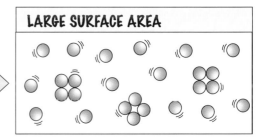

LARGE SURFACE AREA

- ... resulting in an INCREASED NUMBER OF COLLISIONS, and an INCREASED RATE OF REACTION.
- Reactions can only take place at the exposed, outer surface of the solid.

4. The Use Of A Catalyst

A catalyst is a substance which ...
- ... INCREASES THE RATE OF A CHEMICAL REACTION, WITHOUT BEING USED UP IN THE PROCESS.
- CATALYSTS are SPECIFIC, i.e. DIFFERENT REACTIONS NEED DIFFERENT CATALYSTS.

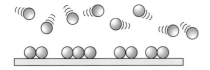

A catalyst lowers the amount of energy needed for a successful collision - so more collisions will be successful and the reaction will be faster. Also it provides a surface for the molecules to attach to, thereby increasing their chances of bumping into each other.

Changing Surface Area

It is important that industrial chemists are able to control the rate of a chemical reaction.

• TOO SLOW - and the process is uneconomical.

• TOO FAST - and the process could be dangerous!

One very simple way of altering the rate of a reaction is to change the SURFACE AREA of any solid reactants.

Demonstration

Limestone (calcium carbonate) and Hydrochloric Acid

Calcium Carbonate + Hydrochloric Acid ⟶ Calcium Chloride + Water + Carbon Dioxide

$CaCO_{3(s)}$ + $2HCl_{(aq)}$ ⟶ $CaCl_{2(aq)}$ + $H_2O_{(l)}$ + $CO_{2(g)}$

We can measure the rate of this reaction by measuring the amount of gas given off every minute.

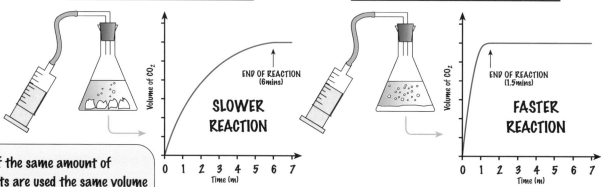

ONCE WITH LIMESTONE CHIPS

END OF REACTION (6mins)

SLOWER REACTION

ONCE WITH LIMESTONE POWDER

END OF REACTION (1.5mins)

FASTER REACTION

NOTE: If the same amount of reactants are used the same volume of gas is produced! It's just that it takes different amounts of time.

We can see that the reaction with powder is faster.

Surface Area And Particle Size

DO NOT CONFUSE THE SURFACE AREA WITH PARTICLE SIZE.

LARGE particles have a SMALL surface area, in relation to their volume.

and so react MORE SLOWLY.

SMALL particles have a LARGE surface area, in relation to their volume.

and so react MORE QUICKLY.

= SURFACE AREA

A large surface area means that more particles are exposed and available for COLLISIONS - this means more collisions and so a faster reaction.

Why should a farmer use powdered limestone to neutralise the acid in the soil - rather than large pieces of limestone?

Changing Concentration

A second way of altering the rate of a chemical reaction is by changing the CONCENTRATION of the reacting solution.

A CONCENTRATED solution is one in which lots of solute particles are dissolved.
e.g. Concentrated sugar solution.

A DILUTE solution is one in which only a small amount of solute particles are dissolved.
e.g. dilute sugar solution.

CLOSE UP VIEW

In a concentrated solution - the particles are crowded close together.

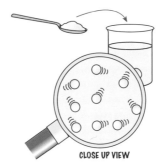

CLOSE UP VIEW

In a dilute solution - the particles are spaced throughout the solvent.

- The more concentrated a solution is, the closer together the particles are. This makes them more likely to bump into one another resulting in faster reactions.

Demonstration

Hydrochloric Acid and Sodium Thiosulphate

Hydrochloric Acid + Sodium Thiosulphate ⟶ Sodium Chloride + Sulphur + Sulphur Dioxide + Water

As the yellow Sulphur is produced the solution becomes cloudy. We can measure the rate of the reaction by timing how long it takes for a cross drawn under the flask to disappear. We can repeat this for different concentrations of acid.

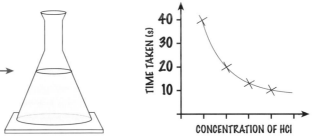

As we increase the concentration of the Hydrochloric Acid, the time taken for the cross to disappear decreases i.e. the reaction is faster.

Pressure

We see a similar effect when the reactants are GASES. As we increase the pressure on a gas, we push the particles closer together - they will then collide more often and the reaction will be faster.

LOW PRESSURE ⟶ RATE OF REACTION INCREASES ⟶ HIGH PRESSURE

Changing Temperature

A third way of altering the rate of a chemical reaction is by changing the TEMPERATURE of the reactants.

- In a COLD reaction mixture the particles are moving quite SLOWLY - the particles will collide with each other less often, with less energy, and less collisions will be successful.

- If we HEAT the reaction mixture the particles will move more QUICKLY - the particles will collide with each other more often, with greater energy, and many more collisions will be successful.

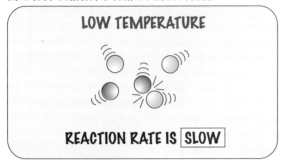

LOW TEMPERATURE

REACTION RATE IS SLOW

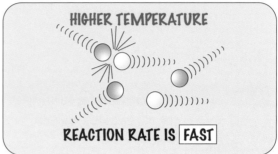

HIGHER TEMPERATURE

REACTION RATE IS FAST

Demonstration

In the HYDROCHLORIC ACID AND SODIUM THIOSULPHATE REACTION we can change the rate of the reaction by heating the solution.

- A small increase in temperature - about 10°C ...
- ... causes a large decrease in the time taken for the reaction to end.
- We can repeat this for different temperatures and plot a graph.
- The reaction goes faster as the temperature increases.

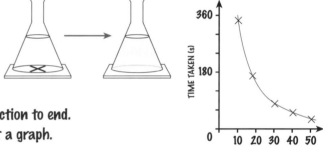

Refrigeration

Why do we keep food in the fridge or the freezer?

- Food deteriorates over time and this deterioration process is a chemical reaction, caused by microbes which work best at 37°C.
- If we keep the food COLD the deterioration process will be SLOWER and the food will keep for longer.
- In the fridge food lasts for several DAYS. In the freezer it can last for MONTHS.
- If milk is left out of the fridge on a HOT day it will go off very QUICKLY.

Light

Some chemical reactions are sensitive to light.

The energy from the light gives the particles enough energy to react. These reactions may be very fast.

EXAMPLES:

PHOTOGRAPHIC FILM

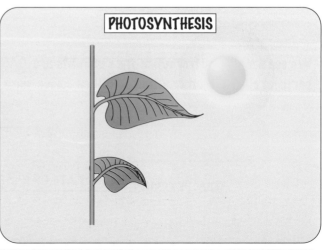

PHOTOSYNTHESIS

Using A Catalyst

A final way of changing the rate of a chemical reaction is by adding a CATALYST.

> A catalyst is a substance which speeds up a chemical reaction without being used up during the reaction.

- Different catalysts are needed for different reactions.

- Because catalysts are not used up, only small amounts of catalysts are needed.

- Catalysts work by reducing the ACTIVATION ENERGY - the minimum energy needed for a reaction to happen.

Demonstration

Decomposition of Hydrogen Peroxide

$$\text{Hydrogen Peroxide} \longrightarrow \text{Water} + \text{Oxygen}$$
$$2H_2O_{2(aq)} \longrightarrow 2H_2O_{(l)} + O_{2(g)}$$

This reaction happens very slowly unless we add a catalyst MANGANESE (IV) OXIDE.
With a catalyst plenty of fizzing can be seen as the oxygen is given off.

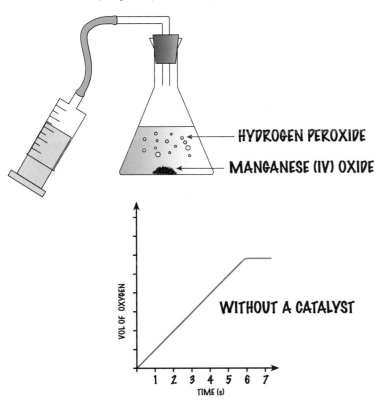

HYDROGEN PEROXIDE

MANGANESE (IV) OXIDE

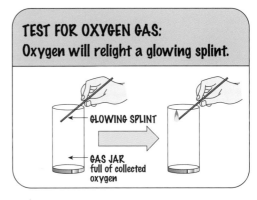

TEST FOR OXYGEN GAS:
Oxygen will relight a glowing splint.

GLOWING SPLINT

GAS JAR
full of collected
oxygen

VOL OF OXYGEN

WITHOUT A CATALYST

1 2 3 4 5 6 7
TIME (s)

VOL OF OXYGEN

WITH A CATALYST

1 2 3 4 5 6 7
TIME (s)

The rate of this reaction could ALSO be changed by changing:

- The CONCENTRATION of the hydrogen peroxide.

- The TEMPERATURE of the hydrogen peroxide.

Catalysts are used a lot in industrial processes to speed up reactions and make production more economical,
but some of the catalysts needed are valuable metals.
Why do you think this doesn't have too much effect on the cost?

Measuring The Rate Of Reaction

Chemical reactions can proceed at different speeds:

- RUSTING is a slow reaction.
- BURNING is a fast reaction.

We can follow the rate of a chemical reaction in TWO ways:

1. Measure the rate at which reactants are used up.

2. Measure the rate at which products are formed ...

    ... e.g. the rate at which a precipitate clouds the reacting solutions.

EXAMPLE:

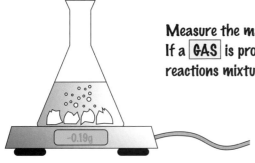

Measure the mass of the reactions mixture. If a GAS is produced the mass of the reactions mixture will decrease.

Measure the volume of gas produced. A gas syringe can be used.

Analysing The Rate Of Reaction

GRAPHS can be plotted to show the progress of a chemical reaction - there are THREE things to remember.

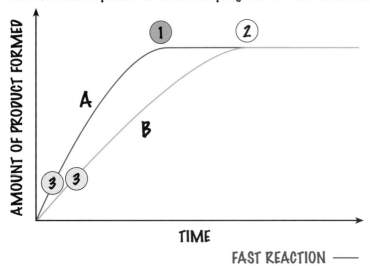

When one of the reactants is used up the reaction stops (line becomes flat).

The same amount of product is formed from the same amount of reactants, irrespective of rate.

The steeper the line the faster the reaction.

REACTION A IS FASTER THAN REACTION B - this could be for one of four reasons:

1. The SURFACE AREA of the solid reactants in A is GREATER than in B.

2. The CONCENTRATION of the solution in A is GREATER than in B.

3. The TEMPERATURE of reaction A is GREATER than reaction B.

4. A CATALYST is used in reaction A but NOT in reaction B.

ENADMES

Enzymes As Biological Catalysts

An **ENZYME** is a biological catalyst. Enzymes control the **RATE OF REACTIONS** in living tissues.

- **SPECIFIC** enzymes are needed for specific reactions within living cells.

The rate of an enzyme catalysed reaction increases with temperature until it reaches about 37°C (body temp.). After this the rate begins to drop and the enzymes become DENATURED (permanently damaged) around 45°C.

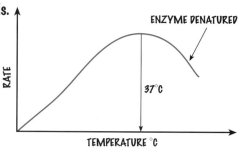

Uses Of Enzymes - Biotechnology

BEER AND WINE

Enzymes in yeast convert the sugar in grapes or grain into carbon dioxide and alcohol - fermentation.

An unwanted by product of fermentation is vinegar.

BREAD

Enzymes in yeast convert the sugar into carbon dioxide which makes the bread rise.

Test for Carbon Dioxide CO_2 - CO_2 turns limewater milky

YOGHURT

Enzymes in bacteria convert sugar in milk (called lactose) into lactic acid.

BANANA YOGHURT

Enzymes can also be used to clarify fruit juice and make soft centred chocolates!

The Lock And Key Mechanism

- Enzymes are **PROTEIN** molecules.

- Each enzyme has a different **SHAPE.**

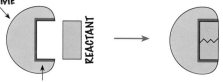

Reactant fits into active site   Reactant is broken down and enzyme can be reused

This is known as the **LOCK AND KEY** mechanism

- Protein molecules are **DENATURED** by **HIGH TEMPERATURES** and **EXTREME pH.**
- If a protein is denatured, it's shape is changed irreversibly and the lock and key mechanism no longer works.

If an enzyme is denatured by heat or extreme pH the reactant no longer fits snugly and cannot be broken down.

- Many **DRUGS** work by **BLOCKING** the active site in an enzyme and **DEACTIVATING** it.

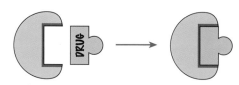

Reversible Reactions

Some chemical reactions are REVERSIBLE - a reversible reaction is one that can proceed in both directions.

$$A + B \rightleftharpoons C + D$$

A and B react to produce C and D, but also C and D can react to produce A and B.

EXAMPLES OF REVERSIBLE REACTIONS:

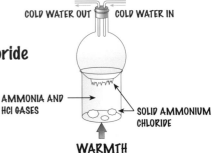
COLD WATER OUT COLD WATER IN

AMMONIA AND HCl GASES

SOLID AMMONIUM CHLORIDE

WARMTH

1. Ammonium Chloride $\rightleftharpoons$ Ammonia + Hydrogen Chloride

$$NH_4Cl_{(s)} \rightleftharpoons NH_{3(g)} + HCl_{(g)}$$

• Solid AMMONIUM CHLORIDE decomposes when heated to give AMMONIA and HYDROGEN CHLORIDE gas.

• HYDROGEN CHLORIDE gas reacts with AMMONIA to give clouds of white AMMONIUM CHLORIDE powder.

2. Hydrated Copper Sulphate $\rightleftharpoons$ Anhydrous Copper Sulphate + Water

$$CuSO_4.5H_2O_{(s)} \rightleftharpoons CuSO_{4(s)} + 5H_2O_{(l)}$$

• Blue crystals of HYDRATED COPPER SULPHATE become white ANHYDROUS COPPER SULPHATE on heating, as WATER is removed.

• If WATER is added to white ANHYDROUS COPPER SULPHATE, blue HYDRATED COPPER SULPHATE is formed and heat is given out.

The Haber Process

Many Industrial Processes are based on reversible reactions -
The HABER PROCESS for the production of AMMONIA is one of them.

Nitrogen + Hydrogen $\rightleftharpoons$ Ammonia

$$N_{2(g)} + 3H_{2(g)} \rightleftharpoons 2NH_{3(g)}$$

The best yield is given by low temperature and high pressure. In other words the conditions in which the reaction occurs can push the equilibrium to the left or right.

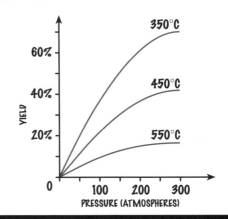
350°C
60%
450°C
40%
YIELD
20%
550°C
0   100   200   300
PRESSURE (ATMOSPHERES)

This affects the yield as can be seen in the graph.

Production Of Ammonia - The Haber Process

The production of Ammonia and Nitric acid are intermediate steps in the production of Ammonium nitrate fertiliser. Until 1908 Nitrogen couldn't be turned into nitrates on a large scale, and the world was quickly running out of fertilisers! Even though air is almost 80% nitrogen!

Fritz Haber showed that Ammonia, a COLOURLESS, PUNGENT, ALKALINE GAS could be made on a large scale.
The Raw materials are:-
● NITROGEN - from the fractional distillation of liquid air.
● HYDROGEN - from Natural gas and steam.

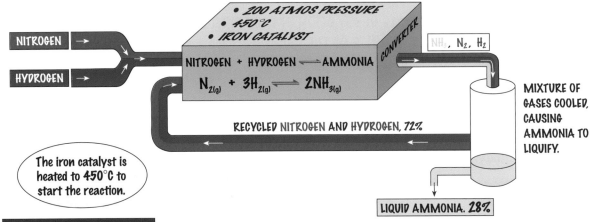

● 200 ATMOS PRESSURE
● 450°C
● IRON CATALYST

NITROGEN + HYDROGEN ⇌ AMMONIA

$$N_{2(g)} + 3H_{2(g)} \rightleftharpoons 2NH_{3(g)}$$

CONVERTER NH_3, N_2, H_2

RECYCLED NITROGEN AND HYDROGEN, 72%

MIXTURE OF GASES COOLED, CAUSING AMMONIA TO LIQUIFY.

The iron catalyst is heated to **450°C** to start the reaction.

LIQUID AMMONIA. 28%

INDUSTRIAL PROCESSES:

Cost depends on ...
● Price of energy.
● Cost of raw materials.
● Wages.
● Equipment.
● Rate of reaction.

Location depends on ...
● Source of raw materials.
● Transport links.
● Source of water.
● Residential areas.

Ammonia Is An Important Chemical

Its main use is in the production of FERTILISERS to increase the nitrogen content of the soil.
Ammonia is also used to produce NITRIC ACID in the following way:

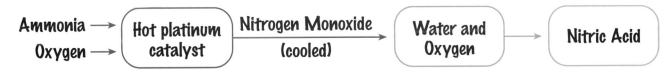

Ammonia →
Oxygen →
Hot platinum catalyst
— Nitrogen Monoxide (cooled) →
Water and Oxygen
→ Nitric Acid

More ammonia can be used to NEUTRALISE the nitric acid to produce AMMONIUM NITRATE - a fertiliser.
AMMONIUM SULPHATE can also be used as a fertiliser.

Plants need nitrogen for healthy growth - but they can't use the nitrogen from the air as it is INERT.
Farmers use artificial fertilisers to replace the nitrogen in the soil, used up by previous crops - so that crop yields can be increased.

● Excessive use of fertilisers can cause problems,
● High nitrate content in drinking water can be harmful.
● Nitrates leaching into lakes and rivers - this causes EUTROPHICATION i.e. ...

Nitrates cause excessive plant growth.

The plants die and start to rot.

The rotting process uses up oxygen and the water cannot support life.

There is great economic importance attached to getting the MAXIMUM AMOUNT of AMMONIA in the SHORTEST POSSIBLE TIME. This demands a degree of COMPROMISE.

Effect Of Temperature And Pressure On The Production Of Ammonia

The manufacture of AMMONIA is a REVERSIBLE REACTION, involving ...

• ENERGY TRANSFERS associated with the breaking and formation of chemical bonds.

$$\text{ENDOTHERMIC} \quad N_2 + 3H_2 \quad \underset{\text{REVERSE}}{\overset{\text{FORWARD}}{\rightleftarrows}} \quad 2NH_3 \quad \text{EXOTHERMIC}$$

In a CLOSED SYSTEM, AT EQUILIBRIUM, ...
  • ... there is the SAME RATE OF REACTION IN EACH DIRECTION ...
  • ... but, the RELATIVE AMOUNTS OF THE REACTANTS depend on ...
      ... the CONDITIONS OF THE REACTION.

EFFECT OF TEMPERATURE 1

Because the formation of ammonia is exothermic, ...

... LOW TEMPERATURE WOULD FAVOUR THE PRODUCTION OF AMMONIA. i.e. favours the forward reaction ...

...which would increase the yield.

EFFECT OF TEMPERATURE 2

Increasing the temperature increases the rate of reaction equally in both directions, therefore ...

... HIGH TEMPERATURE WOULD MAKE AMMONIA FORM FASTER (and break down faster!)

EFFECT OF PRESSURE

Since four molecules are being changed into two molecules, increasing the pressure favours the smaller volume. Therefore ... HIGH PRESSURE FAVOURS THE PRODUCTION OF AMMONIA, ...

... and increases the yield.

A Compromise Solution

In reality, A LOW TEMPERATURE INCREASES YIELD BUT THE REACTION IS TOO SLOW.
So, a COMPROMISE is reached in the Haber process ...

450°C is used as a COMPROMISE SOLUTION.

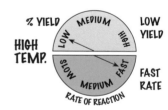

... while also ... CONCENTRATION or in this case PRESSURE also has an important role.
  • INCREASING THE PRESSURE, favours the reaction which results in a reduction in volume ...
  • ... and therefore MOVES THE EQUILIBRIUM to the RIGHT ... INCREASING THE YIELD ...
  • ... as the VOLUME OF AMMONIA PRODUCED is LESS ...
  • ... than the TOTAL VOLUME of NITROGEN and HYDROGEN which react to produce it.

In reality, A HIGH PRESSURE INCREASES YIELD BUT THE REACTION IS TOO EXPENSIVE.
So, yet again, a COMPROMISE is reached ...

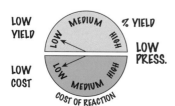

200 ATMOS.PRESS. is used as a COMPROMISE SOLUTION.

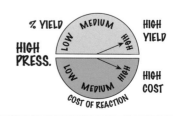

Rates

COLLISION THEORY

- In order for a reaction to take place particles must COLLIDE with sufficient ENERGY.
- The more frequent the collisions the faster the reaction will be.
- The more energy the particles have, the more successful collisions there are and the faster the reaction will be.

CHANGING THE RATE

- SURFACE AREA. Increased surface area means more collisions and a faster reaction.
- CONCENTRATION. Increased concentration means more collisions and a faster reaction.
- TEMPERATURE. Increased temperature means more energetic collisions and a faster reaction.
- CATALYSTS. A catalyst reduces the energy needed for a successful reaction and therefore increases the rate. It is not used up.

ENZYMES

- Enzymes are BIOLOGICAL CATALYSTS.
- Enzymes are DENATURED by high temperatures and extreme pH.
- Enzymes are used in the production of BREAD, WINE AND BEER YOGHURT.

Equilibrium

EQUILIBRIUM IN REVERSIBLE REACTIONS

- Some reactions can proceed in BOTH DIRECTIONS.
- If one direction is EXOTHERMIC the other is ENDOTHERMIC.
- Many INDUSTRIAL PROCESSES are reversible.
- The YIELD depends on the CONDITIONS of the reaction.

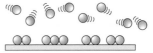

COLD WATER OUT COLD WATER IN

AMMONIA AND HCl GASES

SOLID AMMONIUM CHLORIDE

WARMTH

HABER PROCESS

- Ammonia is produced from Nitrogen and Hydrogen in the HABER PROCESS.
- LOW TEMPERATURES and HIGH PRESSURES favour HIGH YIELD.
- OPTIMUM conditions of 450°C, 200 ATMOSPHERES and an iron catalyst are chosen to make the process as economical as possible - factors to be considered are: YIELD, RATE AND ENERGY COSTS.
- Ammonia is used in the production of NITRIC ACID and FERTILISERS.
- Fertilisers cause increased CROP YIELD.
- Fertilisers cause CONTAMINATED WATER supplies and EUTROPHICATION.

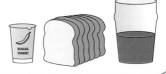

HABER

$N_2 + 3H_2 \rightleftharpoons 2NH_3$

NITRAM FERTILISER

Record the TEN 'Rates' facts and TEN 'Equilibrium' facts onto your tape.
Now - READ, COVER WRITE and CHECK the TWENTY facts.

ACID RAIN

- CO_2, SO_2 and Nitrogen Oxides from car engines are acidic.
- These dissolve to form acid rain.
- Damages lakes, trees + buildings.
- Neutralised by lime or limestone.

ACIDS, ALKALIS AND pH

- Solutions can be acid, alkali or neutral.
- Measured on the pH scale.

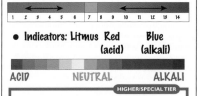

- Indicators: Litmus Red   Blue
                        (acid)   (alkali)

ACID   NEUTRAL   ALKALI

- H^+ - hydrogen ions are in <u>acids</u>
- OH^- - hydroxide ions are in <u>alkalis</u>

NEUTRALISATION + SALTS

- Acid + alkali $\longrightarrow$ salt + water.
- Neutralisation - used to solve indigestion + acidic soil.
- The salt formed depends on the metal in the alkali + the type of acid used.
- Hydrochloric acid produces <u>chlorides</u>.

  Sulphuric acid produces <u>sulphates</u>.

  Nitric acid produces <u>nitrates</u>.

COMBUSTION

- Burning fuels releases carbon dioxide, water and often sulphur dioxide.
- Incomplete combustion produces toxic carbon monoxide.
- Environmental problems - global warming, smog, acid rain.

EXOTHERMIC REACTIONS

- Energy given out to the surroundings.
- Reaction feels hot.
- e.g. Combustion, neutralisation, respiration.

HOT

ENDOTHERMIC REACTIONS

- Energy taken in from the surroundings.
- Reaction feels cold.
- e.g. Photosynthesis, some dissolving processes.

COLD

MEASURING ENERGY CHANGES

- Measured using a thermometer.

HIGHER/SPECIAL TIER

- Energy = mass × specific heat capacity × temperature change.

Energy Changes In Chemical Reactions

HIGHER/SPECIAL TIER

MAKING AND BREAKING BONDS

- In a reaction old bonds must be broken and new ones made.
- Breaking bonds is endothermic as energy must be taken in.
- Making bonds is exothermic as energy is given out.
- The amount of energy taken in compared to the amount given out tells us if the reaction is exo-or endothermic.

HIGHER/SPECIAL TIER

ENERGY LEVEL DIAGRAMS

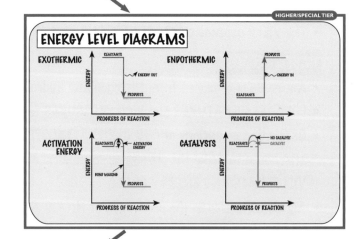

HIGHER/SPECIAL TIER

CALCULATING ENERGY CHANGES

- The amount of energy involved in the making or breaking of bonds is the bond energy.
- These can be used to calculate energy changes. Energy in - energy out = energy change.
- Energy changes can also be measured from energy level diagrams.

Many chemical reactions are accompanied by a temperature change.

Endothermic Reactions

Some reactions are accompanied by a FALL IN TEMPERATURE.
These are known as ENDOTHERMIC reactions because HEAT ENERGY is taken IN from the surroundings.

e.g. Dissolving Ammonium Chloride crystals in water.

$$NH_4Cl_{(s)} \quad + \quad H_2O_{(l)} \longrightarrow \quad NH_4Cl_{(aq)}$$

AMMONIUM CHLORIDE CRYSTALS

AMMONIUM CHLORIDE SOLUTION

The test tube will feel COLD as heat is taken IN from the water.

PHOTOSYNTHESIS and some DISSOLVING processes are endothermic.

Exothermic Reactions

Many reactions are accompanied by a TEMPERATURE RISE.
These are known as EXOTHERMIC reactions because HEAT ENERGY is given OUT to the surroundings.

EXAMPLES:

1. Anhydrous Copper Sulphate + Water ⟶ Hydrated Copper Sulphate + HEAT ENERGY

2. Nitric Acid + Sodium Hydroxide ⟶ Sodium Nitrate + Water + HEAT ENERGY

3. Methane + Oxygen ⟶ Carbon Dioxide + Water + HEAT ENERGY

The last example is COMBUSTION, i.e. burning fuel, perhaps the most obvious exothermic reaction.

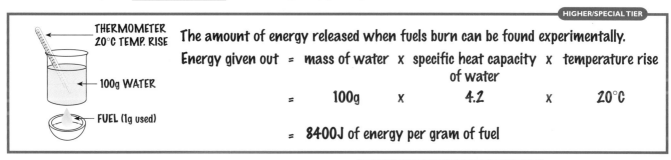

HIGHER/SPECIAL TIER

THERMOMETER 20°C TEMP. RISE

100g WATER

FUEL (1g used)

The amount of energy released when fuels burn can be found experimentally.

Energy given out = mass of water x specific heat capacity x temperature rise of water

= 100g x 4.2 x 20°C

= 8400J of energy per gram of fuel

Some chemicals reactions give out other forms of energy: LIGHT, SOUND or ELECTRICITY.
e.g. when two dissimilar metals react in an electrolyte, electricity is produced.

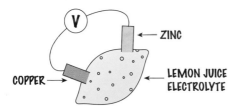

V

ZINC

COPPER

LEMON JUICE ELECTROLYTE

HIGHER/SPECIAL TIER

A FRUIT BATTERY
• The voltage produced depends on the metals used.

Summary

In EXOTHERMIC reactions energy EXITS (hot).

e.g. • COMBUSTION
• NEUTRALISATION
• REPIRATION

In ENDOTHERMIC reactions energy ENTERS (cold).

e.g. • DISSOLVING OF SHERBERT AND AMMONIUM SALTS
• PHOTOSYNTHESIS

We can easily test for these with a THERMOMETER!

Burning Fuels

When fuels burn, energy is released as HEAT - it is an EXOTHERMIC reaction.
• Many fuels are HYDROCARBONS, some may also contain SULPHUR.
• When fuels burn they are reacting with oxygen from the air.
• Reactions with oxygen (oxidation) produce OXIDES.

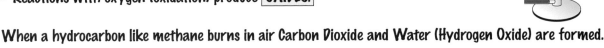

When a hydrocarbon like methane burns in air Carbon Dioxide and Water (Hydrogen Oxide) are formed.

$$\text{Methane} \; + \; \text{Oxygen} \longrightarrow \text{Carbon Dioxide} \; + \; \text{Water}$$
$$CH_{4(g)} \; + \; 2O_{2(g)} \longrightarrow CO_{2(g)} \; + \; 2H_2O_{(g)}$$

We can TEST for these products:
CARBON DIOXIDE - Turns limewater milky.
WATER - Turns BLUE anhydrous Cobalt Chloride paper PINK.

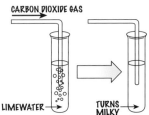

CARBON DIOXIDE GAS

LIMEWATER → TURNS MILKY

If the fossil fuel contains sulphur - sulphur dioxide is formed too.

If a fuel burns without sufficient oxygen, e.g. in a room with poor ventilation, then INCOMPLETE COMBUSTION takes place and CARBON MONOXIDE (a poisonous gas) or CARBON can be formed.

Sooty, yellow flame contains carbon

$$\text{Methane} + \text{Oxygen} \longrightarrow \text{Carbon Monoxide} + \text{Water}$$

$$\text{Methane} + \text{Oxygen} \longrightarrow \text{Carbon} + \text{Water}$$

Effects Of Burning Fuels

We use many hydrocarbon fuels to drive internal combustion engines in cars, here the HEAT energy that is given out is converted into MOVEMENT energy.

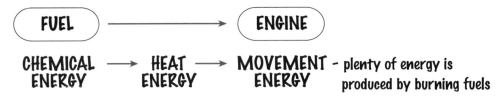

FUEL ⟶ ENGINE

CHEMICAL → HEAT → MOVEMENT - plenty of energy is
ENERGY   ENERGY   ENERGY   produced by burning fuels

Because combustion reactions produce so many gases - the earth's atmosphere is changed.
• CARBON DIOXIDE - greenhouse effect/global warming.
• SULPHUR DIOXIDE - Acid rain.
• *NITROGEN OXIDES - Acid rain/photochemical smog.
  *The high temperatures in car engines can cause Nitrogen and Oxygen in the air to react forming Nitrogen Oxides.

This exothermic reaction is very important to us - it provides us with heat, cooking, transport and many other things that we couldn't do without - but the pollution that it causes means that we must try to cut down the amount of fuel that we burn.

• Catalytic converters can reduce some unwanted emissions like carbon monoxide, nitrogen oxide and unburnt hydrocarbons.

Formation Of Acid Rain

When FUELS burn, oxides form of the elements that they contain.

• Fuels contain non-metals, and most NON-METAL OXIDES are ACIDIC when dissolved in water.

Fossil Fuels contain ...

• ... CARBON - which oxidises to CARBON DIOXIDE.

• ... HYDROGEN - which oxidises to WATER (this is neutral).

• ... SULPHUR - which oxidises to SULPHUR DIOXIDE.

• Combustion engines also cause nitrogen + oxygen in the air to combine to form - NITROGEN OXIDES.

• Carbon dioxide, nitrogen oxides and especially sulphur dioxide are ACIDIC gases.

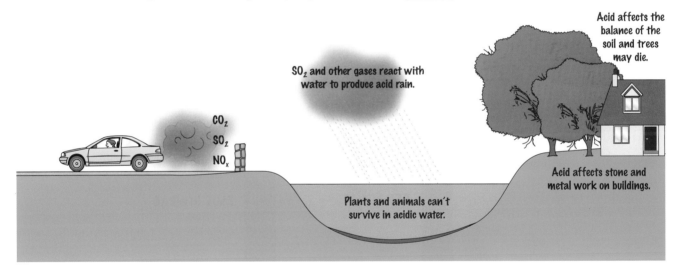

Acid affects the
balance of the
soil and trees
may die.

SO_2 and other gases react with
water to produce acid rain.

CO_2
SO_2
NO_x

Acid affects stone and
metal work on buildings.

Plants and animals can't
survive in acidic water.

• Acid rain is a combination of acids including sulphuric acid from sulphur dioxide.

$$\text{Sulphur Dioxide} + \text{Water} + \text{Oxygen} \longrightarrow \text{Sulphuric Acid}$$

Lessening The Effects Of Acid Rain

Acids in rivers, lakes and soil has to be NEUTRALISED to prevent these harmful effects.

• LIMESTONE - Calcium Carbonate ...

• ... or LIME - Calcium Oxide are often used.

$$\text{Calcium Carbonate} + \text{Sulphuric Acid} \longrightarrow \text{Calcium Sulphate} + \text{Water} + \text{Carbon Dioxide}$$
$$CaCO_{3(s)} + H_2SO_{4(aq)} \longrightarrow CaSO_{4(s)} + H_2O_{(l)} + CO_{2(g)}$$

$$\text{Calcium Oxide} + \text{Sulphuric Acid} \longrightarrow \text{Calcium Sulphate} + \text{Water}$$
$$CaO_{(s)} + H_2SO_{4(aq)} \longrightarrow CaSO_{4(s)} + H_2O_{(l)}$$

pH Scale

- When a substance dissolves in water it forms an AQUEOUS solution.
- The solution may be ACIDIC, ALKALINE OR NEUTRAL.
- Water itself is neutral.

The pH scale is a measure of the acidity or alkalinity of an aqueous solution.

VERY ACIDIC	←	→	SLIGHTLY ACIDIC	NEUTRAL	SLIGHTLY ALKALINE	←	→	VERY ALKALINE
1	2	3	4	5	6	7	8	9	10	11	12	13	14

EXAMPLES:

	HYDROCHLORIC ACID	STOMACH ACID	VINEGAR	MILK	WATER	TOOTHPASTE	LIMEWATER	AMMONIA	SODIUM HYDROXIDE
pH	1	2	4	6	7	8	10	12	14

Indicators

- Indicators can be used to show whether a solution is acidic, alkaline or neutral by the way their colours change.
- LITMUS - has two colours.

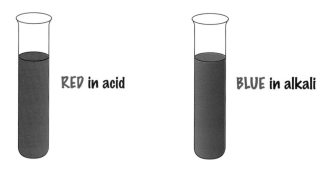

RED in acid   BLUE in alkali

- UNIVERSAL INDICATOR - has a range of colours from acid through neutral to alkali.

| 1 | 2 | 3 | 4 | 5 | 6 | 7 | 8 | 9 | 10 | 11 | 12 | 13 | 14 |

HIGHER/SPECIAL TIER

Ions

- When substances dissolve in water, they dissociate into their individual IONS.
- Alkalis in solution contain HYDROXIDE ions, $OH^-_{(aq)}$
  (alkalis are soluble BASES).
- Acids in solution contain HYDROGEN ions. $H^+_{(aq)}$
- When equal amounts of acid and alkali are combined the hydroxide ions and the hydrogen ions react together to form WATER which is neutral. This is known as NEUTRALISATION.

$$H^+_{(aq)} + OH^-_{(aq)} \longrightarrow H_2O_{(l)}$$

$$Acid + Alkali \longrightarrow Neutral$$

Neutralisation

When an acid and alkali react together a NEUTRAL solution of a SALT and WATER is produced.
- This reaction is exothermic and is called NEUTRALISATION.

$$Acid + Alkali \longrightarrow Salt + Water$$

- We often need to neutralise acids and alkalis.

EXAMPLES:

- Indigestion is caused by excess ACID in the stomach. It can be neutralised by taking a tablet containing an ALKALI.

- Acidic soil can be neutralised by the addition of lime - an alkaline substance.

- Bee stings are acidic and Wasp stings are alkaline - how could the pain be relieved?

Preparation Of Salts

The particular salt produced in a neutralisation reaction depends on:
- THE METAL IN THE ALKALI.
- THE ACID USED.

	HYDROCHLORIC ACID	SULPHURIC ACID	NITRIC ACID
+ SODIUM HYDROXIDE	→ SODIUM CHLORIDE + WATER	→ SODIUM SULPHATE + WATER	→ SODIUM NITRATE + WATER
+ POTASSIUM HYDROXIDE	→ POTASSIUM CHLORIDE + WATER	→ POTASSIUM SULPHATE + WATER	→ POTASSIUM NITRATE + WATER
+ CALCIUM HYDROXIDE	→ CALCIUM CHLORIDE + WATER	→ CALCIUM SULPHATE + WATER	→ CALCIUM NITRATE + WATER

When a neutral solution of salt and water has been produced the salt can be recovered by:
- Evaporating the solution until a saturated solution is formed (crystals form around the edge of the dish).
- Leaving the solution to crystalise overnight.

- Some metal oxides and hydroxides (e.g. those of K, Na and Ca) dissolve in water to produce alkalis.

- Soluble oxides of non-metals (e.g. those of Carbon, Sulphur and Nitrogen) produce acidic solutions.

Other Methods Of Producing Salts

Acids such as hydrochloric acid and sulphuric acid undergo the following reactions to produce salts.

Acid + Metal ⟶ Salt + Hydrogen

Acid + Metal Oxide (or hydroxide) ⟶ Salt + Water

YOU REALLY NEED TO LEARN THESE BY HEART

Acid + Metal Carbonate (or hydrogen carbonate) ⟶ Salt + Water + Carbon Dioxide

Acid + Ammonia ⟶ Ammonium Salt + Water

Making And Breaking Bonds

In a chemical reaction new substances are produced. In order to do this the BONDS in the reactants must be BROKEN, and new BONDS in the products must be MADE.

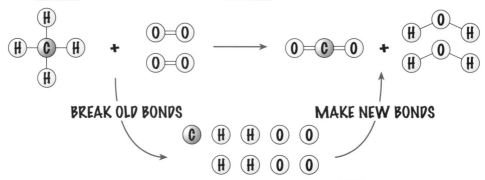

BREAK OLD BONDS   MAKE NEW BONDS

- Breaking a chemical bond is hard work - a lot of energy has to be put IN.
- If energy is going IN this must be an ENDOTHERMIC process.
- When a new chemical bond is made - energy is given OUT.
- As energy is being given OUT this must be an EXOTHERMIC process.
- BREAKING bonds is ENDOTHERMIC, MAKING bonds is EXOTHERMIC.

We can use this idea to find out if a chemical reaction is exo- or endothermic.

ENDOTHERMIC

If MORE energy is NEEDED to break old bonds, than is released when new bonds are made, the reaction must be ENDOTHERMIC.

EXOTHERMIC

If MORE energy is RELEASED when new bonds are made, than is needed to break the old bonds, the reaction must be EXOTHERMIC.

Energy Level Diagrams

The energy changes in a chemical reaction can be illustrated using an ENERGY LEVEL DIAGRAM.

1. Exothermic Processes

In an exothermic reaction energy is given OUT. This means energy is being LOST so the products have less energy than the reactants.

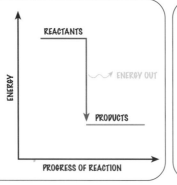

2. Endothermic Processes

In an endothermic reaction, energy is being taken IN. This means that energy is being GAINED, so the products have more energy than the reactants.

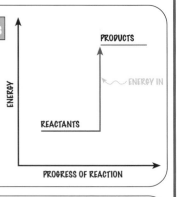

3. Activation Energy

The ACTIVATION ENERGY is the energy needed to start a reaction i.e. to break the old bonds. We can show this on an energy level diagram too.

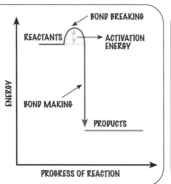

4. Catalysts

CATALYSTS reduce the activation energy for a reaction - this makes the reaction go faster.

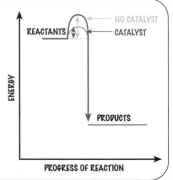

Examples Of Bond Energies

● We have seen that energy is NEEDED to BREAK bonds,
... and energy is RELEASED when MAKING bonds.

The AMOUNT of energy involved when bonds are broken or
made depends on the particular bonds you are dealing with.

We can look up these BOND ENERGIES in data books (you will be
told them in an exam question) and use them to find out how much
energy is taken in or released in a reaction.

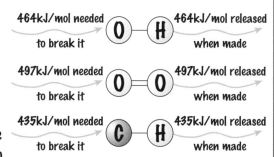

● The units are kilojoules per mole.

Calculating Nett Energy Transfers Using Bond Energies

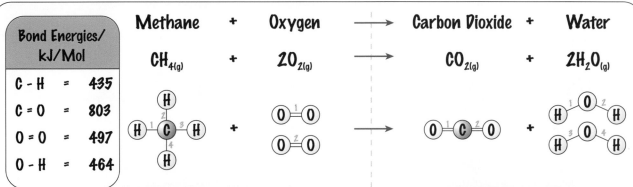

Bond Energies/ kJ/Mol		
C - H	=	435
C = O	=	803
O = O	=	497
O - H	=	464

Methane + Oxygen ⟶ Carbon Dioxide + Water

$CH_{4(g)}$ + $2O_{2(g)}$ ⟶ $CO_{2(g)}$ + $2H_2O_{(g)}$

BONDS TO BE BROKEN
(energy in)

4 x (C - H) + 2 x (O = O)

= (4 x 435) + (2 x 497)

= 1740 + 994

= 2734 kJ/mol

BONDS TO BE MADE
(energy out)

2 x (C = O) + 4 x (O - H)

= (2 x 803) + (4 x 464)

= 1606 + 1856

= 3462 kJ/mol

So 2734 kJ/mol go IN and 3462 kJ/mol go OUT.

The difference is 2734 - 3462 = -728 kJ/mol of energy being given OUT (since it is negative).

This is an EXOTHERMIC REACTION.

Energy Level Diagrams

We can also use energy level diagrams to find the energy change for a chemical reaction.

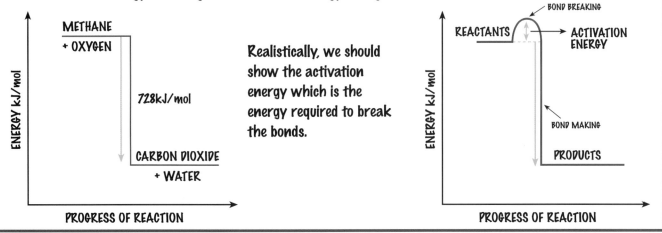

Realistically, we should
show the activation
energy which is the
energy required to break
the bonds.

Chemical Reactions

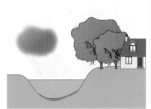

HOT   COLD

EXOTHERMIC AND ENDOTHERMIC REACTIONS

- Chemical reactions are accompanied by energy changes.
- If energy is given OUT, the reaction feels HOT, and is EXOTHERMIC.
- If energy is taken IN, the reaction feels COLD, and is ENDOTHERMIC.

COMBUSTION (AN EXOTHERMIC REACTION)

- When fuels burn in air, OXIDES are produced, CO_2, H_2O and SO_2.
- INCOMPLETE combustion produces CARBON MONOXIDE which is toxic.
- Burning fuels causes environmental problems such as GLOBAL WARMING, SMOG and ACID RAIN.

ACID RAIN

- Carbon dioxide, Nitrogen oxides and especially Sulphur dioxide are ACIDIC GASES.
- When they dissolve in rain water, ACID RAIN is formed which damages LAKES, TREES and BUILDINGS.
- Acid in lakes, rivers and soil can be NEUTRALISED using LIMESTONE or LIME.

ACIDS, ALKALIS AND pH

- Acids and Alkalis are measured on the pH SCALE.
- INDICATORS such as LITMUS and UNIVERSAL INDICATOR can also be used.

ACID   NEUTRAL   ALKALI

HIGHER/SPECIAL TIER

- Acids contain HYDROGEN IONS H^+,
- Alkalis contain HYDROXIDE IONS OH^-.

$$H^+_{(aq)} + OH^-_{(aq)} \longrightarrow H_2O_{(l)}$$

Acid + Alkali $\longrightarrow$ Neutral

NEUTRALISATION AND SALTS

- Acid + Alkali $\longrightarrow$ Salt + Water - this is NEUTRALISATION.
- The SALT produced depends on the METAL IN THE ALKALI and the TYPE OF ACID used.

Energy Changes

HIGHER/SPECIAL TIER

MAKING AND BREAKING BONDS

- MAKING BONDS releases energy - it is EXOTHERMIC.
- BREAKING BONDS takes in energy - it is ENDOTHERMIC.
- If MORE ENERGY is RELEASED from MAKING BONDS than is TAKEN IN from BREAKING BONDS a reaction will be EXOTHERMIC - and vice versa!

ENERGY LEVEL DIAGRAMS

- ENDOTHERMIC

- EXOTHERMIC

- ACTIVATION ENERGY

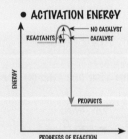

CALCULATING ENERGY CHANGES

- The BOND ENERGY is the energy involved when bonds are made OR broken.
- We can use bond energies to CALCULATE the ENERGY CHANGES for a reaction.
- We can also MEASURE this change as an ENERGY LEVEL DIAGRAM.

Record the FIFTEEN facts on 'Chemical Reactions' and the NINE 'Energy Changes' facts onto your tape.
Now - READ, COVER, WRITE and CHECK the TWENTY FOUR facts.

EVIDENCE FOR TECTONIC THEORY

- Continents fit together.
- Mountain ranges, volcanos and earthquakes at plate boundaries.

TECTONIC THEORY

- Crust is cracked into plates.
- Movement due to convection currents in the mantle.

PLATES MOVE

CONVECTION CURRENTS AS HOT MOLTEN ROCK RISES

EFFECTS OF TECTONIC THEORY

- Earthquakes.
- Volcanos.
- Mountain ranges.

HIGHER/SPECIAL TIER
- Subduction.

HIGHER/SPECIAL TIER
- Sea floor spreading.

EARTH STRUCTURE

CRUST

CORE

MANTLE

SEDIMENTARY ROCK

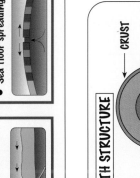

- Formed from grains of weathered rock – sediment.
- Compressed and cemented.
- Layers of grains with fossils.
- Limestone, sandstone.

METAMORPHIC ROCK

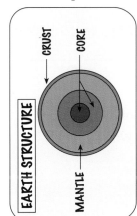

- Old rock is heated and compressed.
- Structure is changed.
- Bands of crystals.
- Slate from mudstone, Marble from limestone.

LIMESTONE

Limestone $CaCO_3$ → Heat → Quicklime CaO

CO_2

Slaked lime $Ca(OH)_2$ ← Water

IGNEOUS ROCK

- Formed from cooling magma.
- Intrusive or extrusive.
- Interlocking crystals.
- Granite.
- Basalt.

Rocks And Tectonics

The Atmosphere

EVOLUTION OF THE ATMOSPHERE

Formation of the Earth — Water condensed — Plants evolved (O_2 Produced) — Nitrogen formed — Ozone layer — New Organisms formed → NOW

FORMATION OF THE EARTH

CO_2, NH_3, CH_4, H_2O

CURRENT ATMOSPHERE

N_2

O_2

KEEPING THE ATMOSPHERE CONSTANT

WATER CYCLE

CARBON CYCLE

NITROGEN CYCLE

GREENHOUSE EFFECT

- Carbon dioxide traps some heat from the sun in our atmosphere.
- We produce too much carbon dioxide from combustion.
- Too much heat trapped causes global warming.

The Changing Gases

The Earth's atmosphere has not always been the same as it is today,
but has gradually evolved over billions of years.

FORMATION OF THE EARTH

Atmosphere consisting mainly of CARBON DIOXIDE
with some AMMONIA, METHANE and
WATER VAPOUR, from volcanic activity.

— 4

WATER VAPOUR condensed to form oceans and seas.

— 3

Plants began to evolve - photosynthesis caused the
atmosphere to be 'polluted' with OXYGEN.

CARBON DIOXIDE reduced by dissolving in oceans
to form carbonates and becoming 'locked-up' in
fossil fuels..

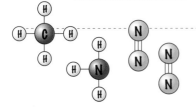

METHANE and AMMONIA reacted with oxygen
in the atmosphere. The reaction with ammonia
producing NITROGEN.

— 2

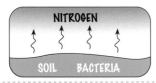

NITROGEN

SOIL   BACTERIA

AMMONIA is converted into nitrates by nitrifying
bacteria and is absorbed by plants or converted
to nitrogen by denitrifying bacteria.

— 1

OXYGEN in the atmosphere resulted in development
of the ozone layer filtering out UV radiation and
allowing new living organisms to evolve.

NITROGEN, N₂   OXYGEN, O₂

Current atmosphere comprises of 78% NITROGEN
21% OXYGEN and small amounts of other gases.

BILLIONS OF YEARS AGO
1 billion = 1000 million

NOW

Oceans

The oceans have also evolved over time as salts from rocks have dissolved in the water.
Salts do not evaporate and have become a permanent part of the oceans.

Composition Of The Atmosphere

Our atmosphere has been more or less the same for 200 million years.

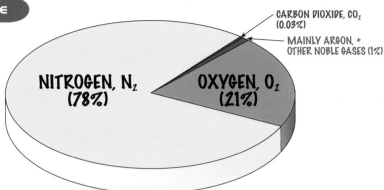

CARBON DIOXIDE, CO₂ (0.03%)

MAINLY ARGON, + OTHER NOBLE GASES (1%)

NITROGEN, N₂ (78%)

OXYGEN, O₂ (21%)

Profile Of The Atmosphere And Atmospheric Pressure

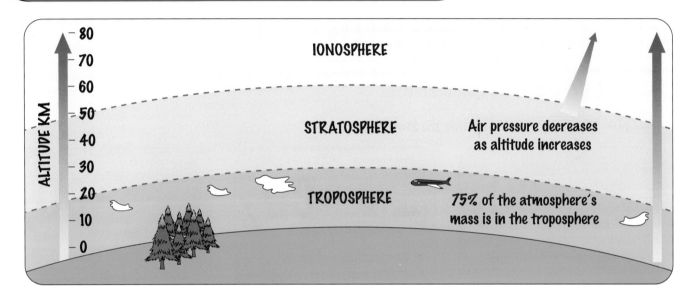

IONOSPHERE

STRATOSPHERE

Air pressure decreases as altitude increases

TROPOSPHERE

75% of the atmosphere's mass is in the troposphere

ALTITUDE KM — 80 70 60 50 40 30 20 10 0

Maintenance Of Our Atmosphere

The atmosphere is kept constant by the following cycles.

WATER CYCLE

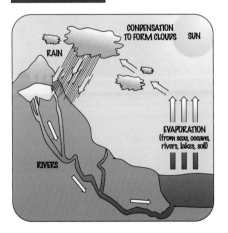

CONDENSATION TO FORM CLOUDS   SUN

RAIN

EVAPORATION (from seas, oceans, rivers, lakes, soil)

RIVERS

The water cycle keeps the water vapour level of the atmosphere constant.

CARBON CYCLE

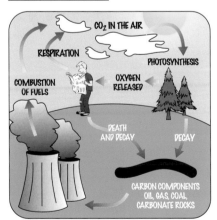

CO₂ IN THE AIR

RESPIRATION

PHOTOSYNTHESIS

COMBUSTION OF FUELS

OXYGEN RELEASED

DEATH AND DECAY

DECAY

CARBON COMPONENTS OIL, GAS, COAL, CARBONATE ROCKS

The carbon cycle helps to keep the oxygen and carbon dioxide levels constant through photosynthesis and respiration. We can upset this balance through excessive combustion.

NITROGEN CYCLE

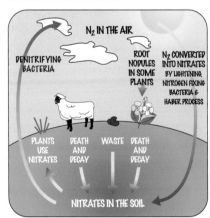

N₂ IN THE AIR

DENITRIFYING BACTERIA

ROOT NODULES IN SOME PLANTS

N₂ CONVERTED INTO NITRATES BY LIGHTENING, NITROGEN FIXING BACTERIA & HABER PROCESS

PLANTS USE NITRATES

DEATH AND DECAY

WASTE

DEATH AND DECAY

NITRATES IN THE SOIL

The nitrogen cycle keeps the nitrogen level of the atmosphere constant.

THE GREENHOUSE EFFECT

The Changing Gases

The Sun is the major source of ENERGY for the Earth
Some gases such as CARBON DIOXIDE are GREENHOUSE GASES.

Light from the sun reaches the Earth and passes through the atmosphere. This warms up the planet which then radiates this heat energy back into space

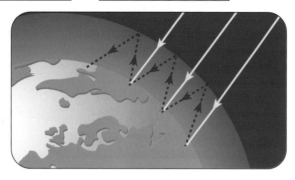

CARBON DIOXIDE helps to trap some of this energy which helps keep the planet warm. Too much carbon dioxide however leads to too much heat being retained; this is GLOBAL WARMING.

Renewal And Release Of Carbon Dioxide

Carbon Dioxide is kept in balance by the CARBON CYCLE. However human activity can upset this balance.

CARBON DIOXIDE IS RELEASED into the atmosphere by:

- Combustion of fossil fuels

- Respiration and decay of plant material

- Action of acid rain on carbonate rock

HIGHER/SPECIAL TIER

CARBON DIOXIDE IS REMOVED from the atmosphere by:

- Photosynthesis

- Solution in Seas (forming calcium and magnesium carbonates)

- Erosion of carbonate rocks

Upsetting The Balance

By BURNING fossil fuels and cutting down rainforests which remove carbon dioxide by PHOTOSYNTHESIS we upset the balance and increase the amount of carbon dioxide in the atmosphere.

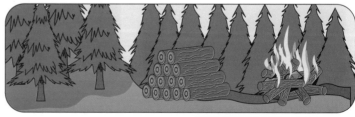

GLOBAL WARMING can cause - melting of icecaps, rising sea levels and flooding - desertification - causing agricultural problems.

A MINERAL is a naturally occurring substance with a definite composition.
A ROCK may consist of one or more minerals.

Igneous Rock

Igneous rock is the first of three main types of rock. Igneous rock is formed as MAGMA (molten rock) which then cools and solidifies, this can happen in two ways.

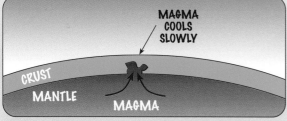

INTRUSIVE IGNEOUS ROCK

MAGMA COOLS SLOWLY

CRUST
MANTLE
MAGMA

When molten rock is forced into the Earth's crust, INTRUSIVE igneous rocks are formed. The rock cools slowly and large interlocking crystals form.

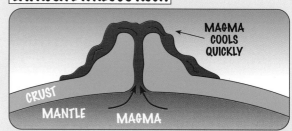

EXTRUSIVE IGNEOUS ROCK

MAGMA COOLS QUICKLY

CRUST
MANTLE
MAGMA

When molten rock erupts from volcanos it forms EXTRUSIVE igneous rock. The rock cools quickly and small interlocking crystals form.

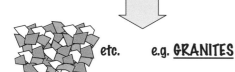

etc.　e.g. **GRANITES**

LARGE interlocking crystals of a VARIETY of minerals with a glassy appearance.

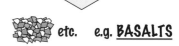

etc.　e.g. **BASALTS**

SMALL interlocking crystals of a VARIETY of minerals with a glassy appearance.

Metamorphic Rock

Metamorphic rock is the second of three main types of rock.

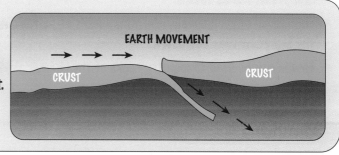

Tectonic activity can cause rocks of all types to be buried deep underground - there they are COMPRESSED and HEATED. This may change the texture and structure of the rock without melting it.

Rocks changed in this way are called METAMORPHIC ROCKS.

EARTH MOVEMENT

CRUST　　CRUST

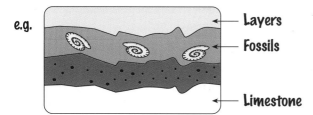

e.g.　← Layers

← Fossils

← Limestone

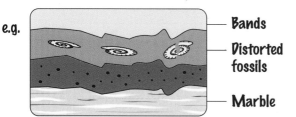

e.g.　← Bands

← Distorted fossils

← Marble

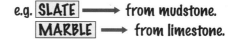

e.g. SLATE ⟶ from mudstone.
MARBLE ⟶ from limestone.

- Metamorphic rocks are BANDED . The bands consist of INTERLOCKING CRYSTALS and the rock is hard. Metamorphic rocks can often be split (cleaved) along their bands.

- Metamorphic rocks are often found in present day ancient mountain belts. They are evidence of the high temperatures and pressure created by mountain building processes.

Sedimentary Rock

Sedimentary rock is the third of the three main rock types.

FRAGMENTS OF ROCK ARE WEATHERED AND WASH INTO STREAMS

THESE FRAGMENTS ARE CARRIED ALONG STREAMS AND RIVERS

WHEN THE WATER REACHES LAKES OR SEAS, THE FRAGMENTS SINK TO THE BOTTOM AS SEDIMENT

SEDIMENTARY ROCK is formed from layers of SEDIMENT deposited one on top of the other. Their WEIGHT squeezes out the water and the particles become CEMENTED together by salts crystallising out of this water. This often takes MILLIONS OF YEARS.

e.g. SANDSTONE from grains of sand.
LIMESTONE from shelly remains of living organisms.

— Layers
— Fossils
— Grains

- Rocks composed of layers of cemented grains or fragments are usually SEDIMENTARY.
- Sedimentary rocks sometimes contain FOSSILS.
- As sediments are laid down, fragments of PLANTS AND ANIMALS may become trapped and preserved as fossils.
- Each layer of rock usually contains fossils of plants and animals that lived at the time the sediment was laid down.
- Fossils can be used to identify rocks of the SAME AGE in different places and to decide which rocks are younger or older than the others.

Identifying Rocks

A simple key like this one can be used to identify the three main types of rock.

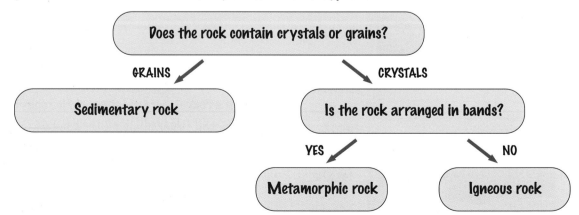

Does the rock contain crystals or grains?

GRAINS

CRYSTALS

Sedimentary rock

Is the rock arranged in bands?

YES

NO

Metamorphic rock

Igneous rock

The Classical Diagram

The formation of the three main types of rock can be summarised by the Rock Cycle.

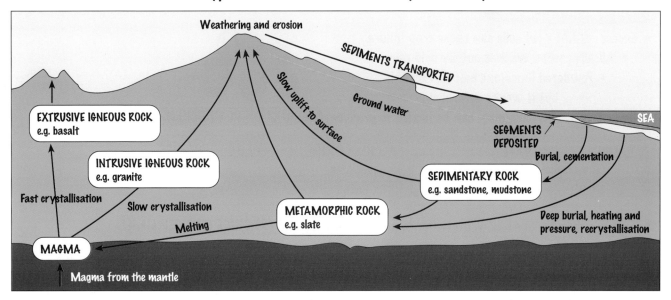

Weathering and erosion

SEDIMENTS TRANSPORTED

Slow uplift to surface

Ground water

SEA

EXTRUSIVE IGNEOUS ROCK
e.g. basalt

SEGMENTS DEPOSITED

Burial, cementation

INTRUSIVE IGNEOUS ROCK
e.g. granite

SEDIMENTARY ROCK
e.g. sandstone, mudstone

Fast crystallisation

Slow crystallisation

METAMORPHIC ROCK
e.g. slate

Deep burial, heating and pressure, recrystallisation

Melting

MAGMA

Magma from the mantle

Weathering

An important part of the rock cycle is WEATHERING and erosion
- the breaking up of rock into small fragments.
This happens in several ways:

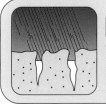

PHYSICAL WEATHERING
water freezes and expands in cracks forcing the rock apart.

CHEMICAL WEATHERING
acid rain reacts with rocks such as limestone.

BIOLOGICAL WEATHERING
roots of plants forces rocks apart.

EROSION
rocks worn away by rain, wind and the action of the sea.

Rock Record

If we look at a cross section of rock we can see evidence of the processes involved in the rock cycle
and the times at which they occurred - this is the rock record.

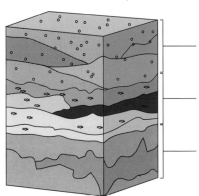

YOUNGEST ROCK
- Sandstone.
- Maybe formed in a desert environment.

MIDDLE ROCK
- Shale, mudstone.
- Formed in a river delta environment.

OLDEST ROCK
- Limestone.
- Formed from shelly remains including fossils, indicates the area was covered by sea.

Limestone is a SEDIMENTARY ROCK consisting mainly of CALCIUM CARBONATE.
It is cheap, easy to obtain and has many uses:

Neutralising Agent

- Excess ACIDITY of soils can cause crop failure.
  - Alkalis can be 'washed out' by acid rain.
    - Powdered limestone can correct this ...
      - ... but it works quite slowly.
- However Calcium Carbonate can be heated to produce CALCIUM OXIDE (QUICKLIME).

CALCIUM CARBONATE ——HEAT——▶ CALCIUM OXIDE + CARBON DIOXIDE
(limestone)   (quicklime)

$$CaCO_{3(s)} \xrightarrow{\text{HEAT}} CaO_{(s)} + CO_{2(g)}$$

- This can then be 'SLAKED' with water to produce CALCIUM HYDROXIDE (SLAKED LIME).

CALCIUM OXIDE ——WATER——▶ CALCIUM HYDROXIDE
(quicklime)   (slaked lime)

$$CaO_{(s)} + H_2O_{(l)} \longrightarrow Ca(OH)_{2(s)}$$

- This, being a HYDROXIDE is quite strongly ALKALINE ...
  - ... and so can neutralise soils and lakes ...
    - ... much faster than just using ...
      - ... powdered limestone.

Building Material

- Limestone can be QUARRIED and cut ...
  - ... into BLOCKS and used directly ...
    - ... to build WALLS of houses ...
      - ... in regions where it is plentiful!
        - It is badly affected by ACID RAIN ...
          - ... but this takes a long time.

Glass Making

- Glass is made by mixing ...
  - ... LIMESTONE, SAND and ...
    - ... SODA (sodium carbonate) ...
      - ... and heating the mixture until it melts.
        - When cool it is TRANSPARENT.

LIMESTONE + SAND + SODA ——HEAT——▶ GLASS

Cement Making

- Powdered limestone and powdered CLAY ...
  - ... are roasted in a ROTARY KILN ...
    - ... to produce dry cement.
      - When the cement is mixed with WATER, SAND and GRAVEL (crushed rock) ...
        - ... a slow reaction takes place where ...
          - ... a HARD, STONE-LIKE BUILDING MATERIAL ...
            - ... called CONCRETE is produced.

CEMENT

Earth's Structure

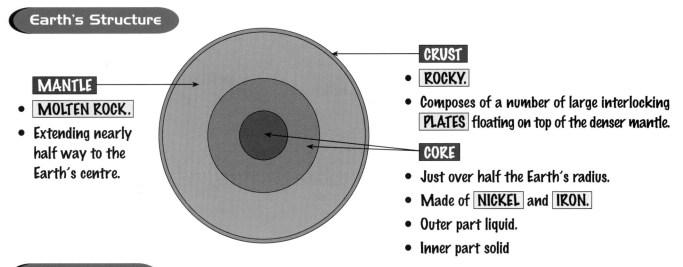

MANTLE
- **MOLTEN ROCK.**
- Extending nearly half way to the Earth's centre.

CRUST
- **ROCKY.**
- Composes of a number of large interlocking **PLATES** floating on top of the denser mantle.

CORE
- Just over half the Earth's radius.
- Made of **NICKEL** and **IRON.**
- Outer part liquid.
- Inner part solid

Tectonic Plates

The Earth's crust is cracked into a number of large pieces called **TECTONIC PLATES** which are constantly **MOVING** at speeds of a few centimeters per year.

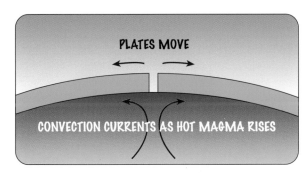

PLATES MOVE

CONVECTION CURRENTS AS HOT MAGMA RISES

- The movement is a result of **CONVECTION CURRENTS** within the Earth's mantle.
- The currents are a result of heat released by natural **RADIOACTIVE PROCESSES** within the Earth.

Evidence For Tectonic Theory

At one time it was believed that the main features of the Earth's crust (mountains etc.) were formed as the Earth cooled and shrank.

Here is the evidence for the current **TECTONIC THEORY.**

200 MILLION YEARS AGO.

- This large land mass is called 'pangaea' by geologists.

PRESENT DAY.

- The coastlines of South America and Africa seem to fit together.
- Similar fossils and rock formations are found on these coasts.
- Mountain ranges exist along plate boundaries.

The 'plates' on the previous page can basically only do THREE things.

1. Slide Past Each Other

- When plates SLIDE, HUGE STRESSES AND STRAINS build up in the crust ...
- ... which eventually have to be RELEASED in order that MOVEMENT can occur.
- This 'release' of energy results in an EARTHQUAKE, the intensity of which may vary but the epicentre will be at the point of greatest realignment.
- A classic example of this is the West Coast of North America (esp. California).

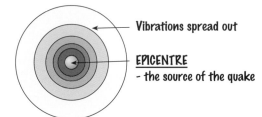

Vibrations spread out

EPICENTRE
- the source of the quake

2. Move Away From Each Other - Constructive Plate Margins

- New rock is formed on the ocean floor at ⟨MID OCEANIC RIDGES⟩ ...
- ... by MAGMA, in rising CONVECTION CURRENTS starting to cool ...
- ... and spread outwards forming new BASALTIC OCEAN CRUST ...
- ... at a rate of about 2cm PER YEAR.
- As the magma cools, IRON-RICH minerals ORIENTATE themselves ...
- ... in the DIRECTION OF THE EARTH'S MAGNETIC FIELD ...
- ... forming ⟨MAGNETIC REVERSAL PATTERNS⟩ ...
- ... parallel to the MID OCEANIC RIDGE.
- The magnetic field of the earth has changed NINE times in the past 3.6 million years, and ...
- ... this is 'mirrored' in these REVERSAL PATTERNS.

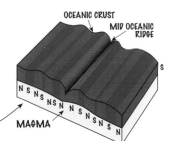

OCEANIC CRUST

MID OCEANIC RIDGE

S

MAGMA

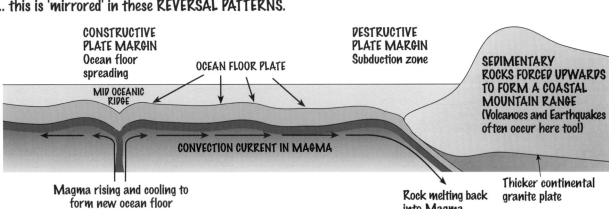

CONSTRUCTIVE PLATE MARGIN
Ocean floor spreading

OCEAN FLOOR PLATE

DESTRUCTIVE PLATE MARGIN
Subduction zone

SEDIMENTARY ROCKS FORCED UPWARDS TO FORM A COASTAL MOUNTAIN RANGE (Volcanoes and Earthquakes often occur here too!)

MID OCEANIC RIDGE

CONVECTION CURRENT IN MAGMA

Magma rising and cooling to form new ocean floor (only a few cm. per year though!)

Rock melting back into Magma

Thicker continental granite plate

3. Move Towards Each Other - Destructive Plate Margins

- As plates are moving away from each other in some places ...
- ... it follows that they must be MOVING TOWARDS EACH OTHER in other places.
- This results in the THINNER, DENSER, OCEANIC PLATE being FORCED DOWN ⟨SUBDUCTED⟩ beneath ...
- ... the THICKER CONTINENTAL GRANITE PLATE, where it MELTS back into the MAGMA.
- This ⟨SUBDUCTION⟩ forces continental crust upwards to form MOUNTAINS and even VOLCANOS ...
- ... and EARTHQUAKES are common e.g. West Coast of South America (Andes).
- N.B. Only OCEANIC PLATES are SUBDUCTED(!!!!) AND RECYCLED INTO THE MAGMA.

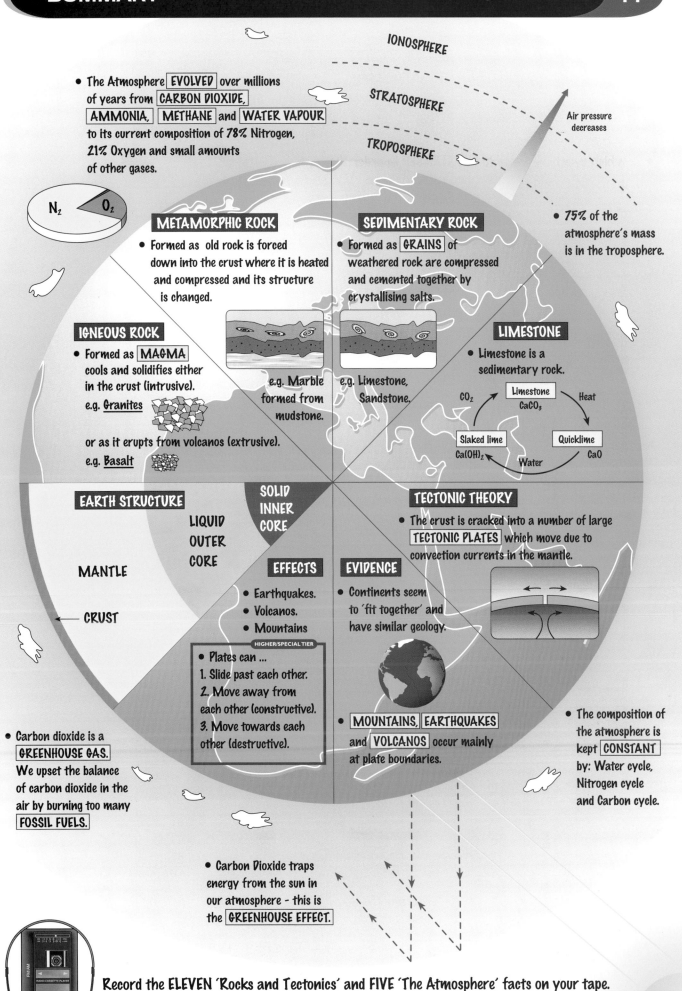

- The Atmosphere EVOLVED over millions of years from CARBON DIOXIDE, AMMONIA, METHANE and WATER VAPOUR to its current composition of 78% Nitrogen, 21% Oxygen and small amounts of other gases.

N_2 O_2

IONOSPHERE

STRATOSPHERE

TROPOSPHERE

Air pressure decreases

- 75% of the atmosphere's mass is in the troposphere.

METAMORPHIC ROCK

- Formed as old rock is forced down into the crust where it is heated and compressed and its structure is changed.

e.g. Marble formed from mudstone.

SEDIMENTARY ROCK

- Formed as GRAINS of weathered rock are compressed and cemented together by crystallising salts.

e.g. Limestone, Sandstone,

IGNEOUS ROCK

- Formed as MAGMA cools and solidifies either in the crust (intrusive).
  e.g. Granites

or as it erupts from volcanos (extrusive).
  e.g. Basalt

LIMESTONE

- Limestone is a sedimentary rock.

CO_2 → Limestone $CaCO_3$ → Heat

Slaked lime $Ca(OH)_2$ ← Water ← Quicklime CaO

EARTH STRUCTURE

SOLID INNER CORE

LIQUID OUTER CORE

MANTLE

← CRUST

EFFECTS

- Earthquakes.
- Volcanos.
- Mountains

HIGHER/SPECIAL TIER

- Plates can ...
1. Slide past each other.
2. Move away from each other (constructive).
3. Move towards each other (destructive).

EVIDENCE

- Continents seem to 'fit together' and have similar geology.

- MOUNTAINS, EARTHQUAKES and VOLCANOS occur mainly at plate boundaries.

TECTONIC THEORY

- The crust is cracked into a number of large TECTONIC PLATES which move due to convection currents in the mantle.

- The composition of the atmosphere is kept CONSTANT by: Water cycle, Nitrogen cycle and Carbon cycle.

- Carbon dioxide is a GREENHOUSE GAS. We upset the balance of carbon dioxide in the air by burning too many FOSSIL FUELS.

- Carbon Dioxide traps energy from the sun in our atmosphere - this is the GREENHOUSE EFFECT.

Record the ELEVEN 'Rocks and Tectonics' and FIVE 'The Atmosphere' facts on your tape.
Now READ, WRITE, COVER and CHECK the SIXTEEN facts.

THE PERIODIC TABLE

Key

Mass number → 1
Proton number (Atomic number) → 1

1
H
hydrogen

The lines of elements going across are called **periods.**

The columns of elements going down are called **groups.**

I	II	III	IV	V	VI	VII	VIII
							4 **He** helium 2
7 **Li** lithium 3	9 **Be** beryllium 4	11 **B** boron 5	12 **C** carbon 6	14 **N** nitrogen 7	16 **O** oxygen 8	19 **F** fluorine 9	20 **Ne** neon 10
23 **Na** sodium 11	24 **Mg** magnesium 12	27 **Al** aluminium 13	28 **Si** silicon 14	31 **P** phosphorus 15	32 **S** sulphur 16	35 **Cl** chlorine 17	40 **Ar** argon 18
39 **K** potassium 19	40 **Ca** calcium 20	70 **Ga** gallium 31	73 **Ge** germanium 32	75 **As** arsenic 33	79 **Se** selenium 34	80 **Br** bromine 35	84 **Kr** krypton 36
85 **Rb** rubidium 37	88 **Sr** strontium 38	115 **In** indium 49	119 **Sn** tin 50	122 **Sb** antimony 51	128 **Te** tellurium 52	127 **I** iodine 53	131 **Xe** xenon 54
133 **Cs** caesium 55	137 **Ba** barium 56	204 **Tl** thallium 81	207 **Pb** lead 82	209 **Bi** bismuth 83	210 **Po** polonium 84	210 **At** astatine 85	222 **Rn** radon 86
223 **Fr** francium 87	226 **Ra** radium 88						

Transition metals

45 **Sc** scandium 21	48 **Ti** titanium 22	51 **V** vanadium 23	52 **Cr** chromium 24	55 **Mn** manganese 25	56 **Fe** iron 26	59 **Co** cobalt 27	59 **Ni** nickel 28	64 **Cu** copper 29	64 **Zn** zinc 30
89 **Y** yttrium 39	91 **Zr** zirconium 40	93 **Nb** niobium 41	96 **Mo** molybdenum 42	101 **Tc** technetium 43	101 **Ru** ruthenium 44	103 **Rh** rhodium 45	106 **Pd** palladium 46	108 **Ag** silver 47	112 **Cd** cadmium 48
139 **La** lanthanum 57	178 **Hf** hafnium 72	181 **Ta** tantalum 73	184 **W** tungsten 74	186 **Re** rhenium 75	190 **Os** osmium 76	192 **Ir** iridium 77	195 **Pt** platinum 78	197 **Au** gold 79	201 **Hg** mercury 80
227 **Ac** actinium 89									

Lanthanides

140 **Ce** cerium 58	141 **Pr** praseodymium 59	144 **Nd** neodymium 60	147 **Pm** promethium 61	150 **Sm** samarium 62	152 **Eu** europium 63	157 **Gd** gadolinium 64	159 **Tb** terbium 65	162 **Dy** dysprosium 66	165 **Ho** holmium 67	167 **Er** erbium 68	169 **Tm** thulium 69	173 **Yb** ytterbium 70	175 **Lu** lutetium 71

Actinides

232 **Th** thorium 90	231 **Pa** protactinium 91	238 **U** uranium 92	237 **Np** neptunium 93	242 **Pu** plutonium 94	243 **Am** americium 95	247 **Cm** curium 96	247 **Bk** berkelium 97	251 **Cf** californium 98	254 **Es** einsteinium 99	253 **Fm** fermium 100	256 **Md** mendelevium 101	254 **No** nobelium 102	257 **Lw** lawrencium 103

Hazard Symbols

Hazard	Symbol	Examples	Dealing with Spillage
Oxidising substances provide oxygen which allows other materials to burn more fiercely		Potassium Chlorate	Wear eye protection. Scoop the solid into a dry bucket. Rinse the area with water.
Highly Flammable substances easily catch fire.		Ethanol	Shut off all possible sources of heat or ignition. Open all windows to ventilate the area. Soak up the ethanol and dilute with water.
Toxic substances can cause death. They may have their effects when swallowed or breathed in or absorbed through the skin.		Chlorine	Evacuate the laboratory! Open a few outside windows to ventilate the room. Keep all internal doors closed.
Harmful substances are similar to toxic substances but less dangerous.		Iodine	Wear eye protection and gloves. Clear the iodine into a fume cupboard and add to sodium thiosulphate solution.
Corrosive substances attack and destroy living tissues, including eyes and skin.		1. Hydrochloric Acid 2. Sodium Hydroxide	1. Wear eye protection. Neutralise with sodium carbonate. Rinse area. 2. Wear eye protection. Neutralise with citric acid. Rinse area.
Irritants are not corrosive but can cause reddening or blistering of the skin.		Calcium Chloride	Wear eye protection. Scoop up solid and dissolve in water.

* Please note some spillages will be dealt with by laboratory technicians or teachers.

Hazchem Code

Vehicles carrying dangerous goods must display hazard information panels that give information to the fire brigade in case of an accident.

1	**Water Jets** - not often used because it can spread out the liquid and increase its surface area leading to a faster rate of reaction.
2	**Water Fog** - often used by fire brigade
3	**Foam** - used for many flammable liquids which would float on water and run away.
4	**Dry Agent**

Each Number matches a hazardous substance (1270 is petrol).

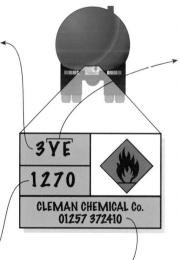

3YE
1270
CLEMAN CHEMICAL Co.
01257 372410

Contact details about the chemical company in case the fire brigade need extra information.

P	V	FULL	
R			
S	V	BA	DILUTE
S		BA for FIRE only	(Dilute with water and
T		BA	wash into drains-not often
T		BA for FIRE only	used because of the
W	V	FULL	environmental impact.)
X			
Y	V	BA	CONTAIN
Y		BA for FIRE only	(Prevent spillage from
Z		BA	entering drains or
Z		BA for FIRE only	waterways.)

E	CONSIDER EVACUATION

V - **Violently** or explosively reactive.

BA - Use **breathing apparatus** and protective gloves.

FULL - Use **full body protective** clothing with breathing apparatus.

INDEX

INDEX

NOTES